Novitiate Reference Library

D1187562

SUMMARY OF SCHOLASTIC PRINCIPLES

**GOOD SHEPHERD CONVENT
ST. LOUIS
PROVINCIAL LIBRARY**

189
WUE

A-581

Summary of Scholastic Principles

BERNARD WUELLNER, S.J.

Department of Philosophy
John Carroll University, Cleveland

Loyola University Press

Chicago 1956

IMPRIMI POTEST
Leo D. Sullivan, S.J.
Provincial, Detroit Province
October 1, 1954

NIHIL OBSTAT
Austin G. Schmidt, S.J.
Censor Deputatus
May 3, 1956

IMPRIMATUR
✠ Samuel Cardinal Stritch
Archbishop of Chicago
May 4, 1956

© 1956, Loyola University Press
Printed in the United States of America
Library of Congress Catalog Card Number: 56-10903
P-MLA-PR-OE

Preface

Principles may well be regarded as the main part of philosophy. They are among the major discoveries of philosophy, condensing in themselves much philosophical inquiry and insight. They are the starting points of much philosophical discussion. They are the base for exposition, for proof, and for criticism. They serve the student and the reader of philosophy much as legal maxims serve jurists and as proverbs serve the people. They are for scholastic philosophers the household truths of their tradition.

All our masters of philosophy know these principles well. They use them as a constant set of convictions and as a standard setting on many subjects. Masters like Aristotle and St. Thomas incessantly weave these principles into their writings, and so much so, that familiarity with their principles becomes an indispensable preparation for any intelligent grasp of their works and for any genuine assent to their conclusions.

The same is true for the better thinkers among nonscholastic philosophers. They have their principles, too, on which hang many of their difficulties and many of their distinctive conclusions. Probably one reason for the bewildering obscurity of the history of philosophy is inattention to the principles of these philosophers, fostered by excessive concentration on their novel views, their special language, and their surprising criticisms.

A little book summarizing these principles for all branches of systematic scholastic philosophy may then prove useful to many undergraduate students. The author has not shunned reasonable repetition since there are sound enough pedagogical reasons to justify repeating for the sake of undergraduates. Repetition is good; repetition in different contexts of related principles is very good; and for students who are still bound by one form of words and who do not notice the close relationships of similar principles, repetition is necessary.

In the main body of this SUMMARY OF SCHOLASTIC PRINCIPLES a consistent pattern of Thomism has been attempted. Disagreements among the scholastics have been noted in a special list (pages 130-36).

The serial numbering system has been used to make reference easier. This does not imply that there are so many hundreds of independent principles, for it is plain that later lists repeat some earlier items and that various principles are either secondary deductions from broader principles or more detailed statements or applications of other formulations of the truths.

Certain omissions are deliberately made because of their controversial nature, and especially because of their less general usefulness to undergraduate students. The logician, for instance, will find no rules on methods of inquiry; the ethician will see no statements on moral standards in taxation; and other philosophers with special interests will discover missing points. The norms for admitting and omitting material were rather pragmatic ones based chiefly on classroom usefulness.

It is outside the scope of this book to discuss the epistemological problems of the origin of our knowledge of principles in general or of particular principles, as that on causality. It is also outside the purpose to discuss the metaphysical or logical meaning, the existential or essential content, and the analogical application of the principles in real instances and individual contexts. Wherever it is true, the existentialist or metaphysical meaning is to be preferred. In his sparkling address to the American Catholic Philosophical Association, "The Genesis and Function of Principles in Philosophy," published in its 1955 *Proceedings* (Volume XXIX), Francis E. Gurr, S.J., has well stated these issues and given an introduction to the literature of the topic.

Every teacher will understand that the exercises offered are only suggestions. The student with initiative will find them helpful. But every good student knows that no book is a substitute for the guidance and recommendations of his teacher.

Table of contents

How to use these materials

The following points may be helpful to undergraduate students in using this SUMMARY OF SCHOLASTIC PRINCIPLES *along with their books in their ordinary philosophy courses. The book has been planned to be helpful in all the systematic courses.*

Learning the principle

The axiom or principle should be so learned that you can state it in its exact and complete form. Accuracy is of great importance in this first learning; accuracy gained in the beginning helps immensely ever afterwards in thinking about or using the principle.

Understanding the principle

Besides remembering the correct wording, you must accurately grasp the meaning of each axiom. This may first require a careful noting of the philosophical terms used in the principle. Then the limitations on the scope and the meaning of each are to be noted. Another help to understanding is to compare the first statement with the variant statements that often are offered; such comparison should show an equivalence or approximation of the variants to the first declaration of the principle. If you do not see this equivalence or closeness of meanings, you probably do not understand the principle but are bound by mere words. Another comparison of principle with principle can be made by checking the cross references given. Thereby you may see the principle in the context of different philosophical topics, so that the different contexts throw light on the meaning of the principle.

Using or manipulating the principle

Illustrate it; apply it to some specific instance; fit it into the particular part of scholasticism that you are currently studying. The several exercises given throughout the text will help you in this way.

Reading about the principle

At the end of each section you will find a body of references for the principles. These references are carefully selected from sources that are thought to be above average in their explanation, use, or proof of the principles referred to. They are well worth your study to deepen your understanding and familiarity with the principles.

Examining the evidence for the principle

Reflect on the validity of each principle. Why is it true? Is it self-evident? Deduced? If so, from what premises or from what other principles? Is it inductively known? Is it analytic? Is it true only in the order of thought or also in the order of reality?

The more advanced student may ask why some of the principles are disputed by certain groups of scholastic philosophers or at least are not regarded as universally true. Those familiar with nonscholastic philosophers may ask which principles are accepted by nonscholastics as well as scholastics. They may also try to understand why nonscholastics challenge some of the scholastic principles or misinterpret others.

Correlating selected principles

The best study of all would be a systematic connecting of relevant principles. Nothing would show greater mastery of the material. An expert sample of such systematic connecting is given in the supplement on the Thomistic theses. Another example is in the exercise on the maxim that activity follows existence. See Exercise 7. Another similar problem would be to find all the principles that would be used in explaining some change such as the start of a bird's singing. Or locate all the references to God in the various principles and see what connections there are between these occurrences. Such tasks can be considerable intellectual fun; they certainly show intellectual initiative.

On the names of principles

Principles are often named from their general subject matter. Thus, an ethical, logical, metaphysical, or psychological principle would refer to a principle belonging to one of these branches of knowledge.

Some principles of frequent occurrence have received special names, usually derived from the topic treated in the principle. Examples are the principle of analogy of being, of finality, and of motion. The general index of principles at the end of the book lists them alphabetically by topics and names.

In the summary given in this book, the principles are grouped conveniently according to major topics, in alphabetical order. The lists begin with *Act and Potency* and run through many topics to the final list on *Will*.

Method of references

All references are given with the full name of the book at its first mention in each chapter. The sequence of references is alphabetical according to authors.

The name of the author is given except for Aristotle and St. Thomas Aquinas. In their case it is presumed that the reader is familiar enough with the corpus of their writing to recognize the author from the name of the work. Citations to the work *On the Soul* are to Aristotle's work unless St. Thomas' disputed question with the same name is explicitly noted.

References to Aristotle are given by book (in roman numeral) and chapter (in arabic numeral). Occasionally, the international index of the locus is also mentioned.

The style of reference to the *Summa Theologiae* is this. Roman numerals refer to parts; arabic numerals following the roman numeral refer to questions; arabic numerals following the hyphen refer to articles within the cited question; *ad* (in reply to) refers to the answers to objections within the article mentioned. When no hyphen is used, the whole question or questions is meant.

The style of reference to the *Contra Gentiles* uses roman numerals for books and arabic numerals for chapters. References to the Disputed Questions (*Truth, On the Power of God, On Spiritual Creatures,* and so on) and to the *Quodlibeta* are made by arabic numbers only, the first number referring to the question and the second, after the hyphen, to the article within the question. *On Being and Essence* is referred to by chapters as given in the edition of Armand Maurer, C.S.B. For less frequently cited works the keys—prologue, distinction, question, article, lecture, and so on— are written out in full.

The number preceding the reference indicates the principle or axiom which is mentioned or discussed in the reference. But the references are not duplicated as the principles are in different contexts and subject headings. For instance, the references to hylemorphism are given only under the primary occurrence of the subject in 255.

There was no need, it seemed, to refer to all the passages in Aristotle and St. Thomas and other writers in which the given principle occurs. Also, no attempt has been made to judge or at least to indicate to the student which is the primary reference among the group given.

Throughout this SUMMARY OF SCHOLASTIC PRINCIPLES full Latin sentences are not printed in italic but in the same roman type as the rest of the text. Isolated Latin words and phrases have been italicized.

Terminology on principles

A principle is that from which anything in any way proceeds; a starting point of being, or of change, or of knowledge, or of discussion.

A principiate is that which proceeds from another in some way. It is the correlative of a principle.

A first principle is one which does not proceed from any prior principle in its own series. Other members of a series between the first principle and the last principiate will be intermediate, derived, secondary, or relatively first principles.

A speculative principle is one directly concerned with truth for its own sake.

A practical principle is one chiefly concerned with activity, whether doing or making.

An ontological or real principle is a being or a part or constituent of a being from which another being or modification of being or a whole proceeds. It is then called a principle of being or of change.

A logical or mental principle is a source of knowledge or of thought; especially, a truth from which another truth or truths proceed or can be learned. It is then called a principle of knowledge. In scholasticism these truths are usually principles about beings. Thus, the principle of causality is a general truth about the need of active real beings to explain the origin of new beings and changes.

Note that a logical principle may be expressed in an ontological or logical formula. (1) The ontological formula states the general truth or definition in terms of being. It is a law of being or existence. (2) The logical formula expresses the general truth or proposition in terms of thought or speech, that is, in terms of concepts, their affirmation, negation, or predication. It is known then as a law of thought. See 32-35 for examples.

Among logical principles, it is helpful to distinguish especially rules, criteria, and signs.

A rule is a guide for action, conduct, evaluation (including interpretation and criticism), and procedure or method. Thus, the principles on conscience are guides for action; the rules on syllogisms are guides for criticism of reasoning; the rules on divine names are guides for right thinking and speech about God's perfections.

A criterion is a standard or test by which a judgment of something else may be formed. Examples in this book are the criteria for just laws, for identifying a cause, for identifying real distinctions.

A sign is that which leads to knowledge of something else.

An axiom or "dignity" is a self-evident, primary truth that is immediately known by us.

A self-evident principle is one that is or can be known immediately, without reasoning or deduction from other principles or experiences.

Examples of principles and principiates

Real principles

Type of principle	Some examples of correlative PRINCIPLES	PRINCIPIATES
1 Beginnings (in time, place, series, position)	January 1 top of a page	a new year rest of the page
2 Origin (without dependence)	God the Father	God the Son
3 Occasions	invitation	attendance
4 Conditions	a clear road	a fast trip
5 Causes		
A efficient cause (agent, maker)	carpenter Congress	door laws
B purpose (final cause, end intended)	man's happiness health	efforts at improvement medical research
c model (exemplary cause, guiding idea)	God's creative plan	order in the universe
D the potency (material cause) from which the thing is produced or deduced	wool wheat, yeast	coat bread
E the form (formal cause, act, formal act)		
1 the substantial form of an essence or nature	soul of man	a living man
2 accidental form	intelligible species of a house	a man thinking of that house
6 Elements of composition	parts or members	a finite whole or a suppositum
A potency and act		
1 in order of being	essence—existence	a finite being
2 in order of essence	prime matter— substantial form organized body—soul	a natural body a living nature
3 in order of operative capacity	substance (nature, essence)—powers	an active being
4 actual operations	powers and acts powers with habits and acts	actual activity
B organic parts	roots, trunks, leaves, and so on	a tree (organized body)
c integral or quantitative parts of material bodies, whether natural or artificial, and mixtures	electrical particles wheels, chassis, motor, and so on letters milk, flavor, starch	atom (natural whole) automobile (artificial whole) a word ice cream

[6

Logical principles

Type of principle	Examples
1 Concepts and definitions	The definitions of change, the good, human act, life, and so on
2 Questions and problems	What is the origin of the world? Problem of the one and the many
3 Signs	Effects as signs of causes The intelligible species
4 General truths or propositions	
A in metaphysics	Act is prior to potency. The end is the principle of the means.
B in logic	The rules of syllogisms
C in ethics	A correct conscience must be obeyed.
D laws of sciences	Laws of levers, of pressures of gases
E mathematical axioms	Parallel lines do not meet.
F precepts of grammar, of rhetoric, and so on	Rules of agreement of relative pronouns
5 Fonts of truth	The senses, immediate concepts, and so on
6 Norms and standards of measurement	The concept of rational nature adequately considered
7 Logical elements of a theory, of a proof, and so on	The premises
8 The starting point of an explanation (This can be the same as 7.)	The roots of words as an introduction to an explanation of their meaning and definition

Exercise 1
Recognizing principles

Directions: A State whether each principle given on the next page is real or logical. B State as far as possible the type or specific name of the principle. The key is on page 137.

Principle	Principiate	Type of principle real or logical	specific name
Examples			
Christmas	church and home feasts	real	occasion
A gun	wounded duck	real	efficient cause (instrumental cause)
Motion begins only when force is applied.	Someone threw that snowball.	logical	general truth of metaphysics and physics

Principles	*Principiates*
1 oil wells	gasoline
2 clues	discovery of a thief
3 persecution	death of martyrs
4 martyrdom	new conversions
5 the title page	the book
6 rules of a syllogism	verifying the correctness of my reasoning
7 the intellectual soul	the human being
8 fogs near icebergs	shipwrecks
9 sight of landing signal	downward drop of plane
10 springtime	new flowers
11 relaxation	his weekly golf game
12 money	the movie industry
13 discovery of radium	discovery of atomic fission
14 emotions	quarrels
15 laws of the United States	federal court decisions
16 light	a good photograph
17 St. Patrick's Day	Irish dancing
18 promotion of justice	formation of governments
19 the eternal law	the natural law
20 his mail	his unpopularity
21 a surgeon's decision	saving a life
22 premises of a proof	the conclusion
23 sugar	jellies
24 melody and tempo	a song
25 solid rock	a safe high building
26 unemployment	crime
27 unemployment assistance	relief laws
28 The end is the measure of the means.	the search for means of family security
29 forests	soil conservation
30 the vital principle	a living body
31 accounting methods	business savings
32 pain	organic disorder
33 relief of pain	administration of morphine
34 arctic flying	progress in meteorology
35 lack of fuses	a fire
36 ringing of the church bells	departure for services
37 rules of real distinctions	refutation of pantheism
38 the virtues of Christ	Christian way of life

1
Act and potency

1 Potency and act constitute a complete and fundamental division of being and of every order of being. *confer* Thomistic thesis 1

Priority (2-4)

2 Act is prior to potency in nature, in excellence, and in intelligibility. Hence, it is said to be absolutely prior to potency.

3 Potency is prior to act in the order of material causality. But it need not be prior in time.

4 Potency can be known and defined only through its corresponding act.

Causal capacities and incapacities (5-11)

5 No potency can actualize itself. A potency can be brought to actuality only by the influence of a being in act. *confer* 51, 86

6 No potency can exist by itself or apart from its composition with act.

7 Every potency has a sufficient reason.
VARIANT No potency is in vain.

8 Potency, both passive and active, is for the sake of act.

9 A thing cannot be in both potency and act with regard to the same thing at the same time.

10 No act can be in potency to itself.
VARIANT No act by reason of its actuality is in potency to a higher degree of its own perfection or its own order of perfection.

11 Howsoever anything acts, it does so inasmuch as it is in act; howsoever anything receives, it does so inasmuch as it is in potency.

Distinction and union of potency and act (12-22)

12 Act and potency in regard to the same perfection must be in the same order and the same category of being.

13 Act and potency in the same order or genus of being stand in contrary and relative opposition to each other, and are therefore really distinct from each other in the being to which they belong.
NOTE By the same order is meant the existential order, the substantial order, the operative order, the accidental order, and so on. See chart on principles and principiates on pages 6-7.

14 *The principle of the limitation of act*: An act or perfection as such is limited only by a potency which is really distinct from it, in which it is received, and with which it unites in a real compound. *confer* Thomistic theses 2-3
Briefly: Act is not limited except by reception in a distinct potency.

15 Every finite act is realized in its proper or proportionate potency. *confer* 169, 379

16 Potency is perfected, specified, and restricted (delimited) by its correlative act.

17 Every changeable being is composed of potency and act as of two intrinsic principles of being. *confer* 50

18 Every finite being is composed of potency and act. *confer* 158

19 Every natural composite being has potency and act as its intrinsic principles.

20 Every individual nature or natural unit, even though a compound, can have only one existential and one substantial formal act. *confer* 256, 512, 537, 550

VARIANTS   A Ex duobus entibus actu non fit unum per se.   B Ex ente potentia et ente actu fit unum per se.

21 Potency and act in the same order of being are transcendentally and immediately related to each other within the being possessing them.

22 Acts of the same kind are multiplied only by the multiple potencies in which they are received, by which they are limited, and with which they are really united.

NOTE   This further extends 14. *confer* Thomistic theses 2-3

Degrees of being (23-24)

23 A thing is perfect to the degree that it is in act, and imperfect insofar as it is in potency. *confer* 209, 228

24 Wherever there is potency, there is some imperfection; wherever there is act, there is some perfection.

Inferences (25-26)

confer 274-81

25 The inference from possibility of being or action to actual being or action is not valid.

26 The inference from actuality of being or action to possibility of being or action is valid.

1-26 REFERENCES

General references: R. Garrigou-Lagrange, O.P., *Reality*, Chapter 5. G. Klubertanz, S.J., *Introduction to the Philosophy of Being* (1955 edition), 101-18. J. Maritain, *Introduction to Philosophy*, Part II, Chapter 7. H. Renard, S.J., *Philosophy of Being* (second edition), Section I, Chapters 1-2

1 *Contra Gentiles*, II, Chapter 54

2-4 *Metaphysics*, IX, Chapters 8-9. *Summa Theologiae*, I, 3-1; I, 9-1

5 *Metaphysics*, IX, Chapter 8. *Summa Theologiae*, I, 2-3 (first way); I, 79-3; I-II, 9-1; I-II, 18-1 *ad* 2

6 *Summa Theologiae*, I, 7-3 *ad* 3

9 *Summa Theologiae*, I-II, 9-3 *ad* 1; I-II, 51-2 *ad* 2

10-12 *Metaphysics,* IX, Chapter 1. *Summa Theologiae,* I, 77-1; I, 115-1. *Contra Gentiles,* I, Chapter 13, "Tertio probat . . ."

14 *Summa Theologiae,* I, 3-4 (second proof); I, 7-1. *Contra Gentiles,* I, Chapter 43, "Amplius . . ."; II, Chapters 52-54. *Compendium of Theology,* I, Chapter 18

15 *Summa Theologiae,* I, 85-7. *Contra Gentiles,* III, Chapter 52 (second proof)

17-19 *Summa Theologiae,* I, 3; I, 9-1, 2; I, 51-2; I, 54-1, 2, 3. *Contra Gentiles,* I, Chapter 18; II, Chapters 51-54. *Quodlibetum,* III, 8

23-24 *Summa Theologiae,* I, 4-1. *Contra Gentiles,* III, Chapter 20 (paragraphs 3-7). *On Being and Essence,* Chapters 4-5

2

Action and passion

27 The action is in the patient or recipient.

28 Action and passion are not really distinct.

29 The agent as agent does not change nor gain nor lose any perfection insofar as it is causing. *confer* 105

30 Action is proportionate to the nature of the agent. *confer* 87D

31 Action and passion are predicated of the suppositum. *confer* 454

27-31 REFERENCES

27 *Physics,* III, Chapter 3. J. A. McWilliams, S.J., *Physics and Philosophy: A Study of Saint Thomas's Commentary on the Eight Books of Aristotle's Physics,* 40-45, 65-67. F. X. Meehan, *Efficient Causality in Aristotle and St. Thomas,* 213-17, 222-28

29 J. A. McWilliams, S.J., "Action Does Not Change the Agent," in J. K. Ryan (editor), *Philosophical Studies in Honor of the Very Reverend Ignatius Smith, O.P.,* 208-21

3

Being

32 *The principle of identity,* ontological formula:
A In terms of existence Whatever is, is.
B In terms of essence Everything has its own essence.
A thing is what it is.

The principle of identity, logical formula:

A The true is true; the false is false.

B The true is to be affirmed; the false is to be denied.

33 *The principle of contradiction,* ontological formula: A thing cannot both be and not be at the same time in the same respect or relation.

VARIANTS A A thing cannot both be *this* and not be *this* at the same time in the same respect or relation. B Contradictories cannot be present together.

NOTE A few authors name this the principle of noncontradiction. In metaphysics being here especially refers to the existing.

The principle of contradiction, logical formula: The same judgment cannot at the same time in the same meaning be both true and false.

VARIANTS A The same attribute cannot at the same time in the same being be truly affirmed and denied of the same subject. B Contradictory judgments cannot be simultaneously true. See inferences from opposition.

34 *The principle of excluded middle,* ontological formula: A thing must either be or not be at the same time in the same respect or relation.

VARIANT There is no intermediate or mean between being and nonbeing nor between any pair of contradictories.

The principle of excluded middle, logical formula: An attribute must be either affirmed or denied of its (corresponding) subject.

VARIANT A proposition must be either true or false.

COROLLARY An inference is either valid or invalid. See 264-70 for other corollaries.

35 *The principle of sufficient reason,* ontological formula:

A There is a sufficient reason or adequate necessary objective explanation for the being of whatever is and for all attributes of any being.

B Full formula: Every being must have either in itself or in another being a sufficient reason for its possibility, actualities, origin, existence and mode of existence, its essence (nature or constitution), its subjective potentialities, powers, habits, operations, changes, unity, intelligibility, goodness, beauty, end, relationships, and any other attributes or predicates that may belong to it.

The principle of sufficient reason, logical formula: Every judgment (affirmative or negative) about a being should have a sufficient reason (that is, sufficient evidence). *confer* 291-92

36 *The principle of intelligibility* (one aspect of the principle of sufficient reason): All that is, is intelligible.
VARIANTS A Every being is ontologically true. B Everything is knowable in as far as it has being or is actual. c The universe is a realm of reason.

37 *The principle of universal analogy*: Any real being is intrinsically analogous to any and every being in the proportion of its essence to its existence.
VARIANT Things exist according to their natures.

38 *Pluralism and hierarchy of perfections of being*:
  A An analogous perfection is not one but many perfections which are found existing in different ways or according to different forms.
  B Wherever there is analogy of perfections, there is diversity of rank or of excellence of the perfections, and vice versa. *confer* 222

39 Every real complete being is an individual substance. *confer* 511

Priority of being (40-44)

40 Being is prior to nonbeing.

41 Existence is the first of all acts, or the act of all actualities or perfections.
VARIANT Being is the actuality of every form or nature.

42 Existence is prior to change.

43 Being is prior to relation of being to being. *confer* 475

44 Being is prior to the true. *confer* 528

32-44 REFERENCES
32-34 *Metaphysics,* IV, Chapters 3-8; XI, Chapters 4-6. *Posterior Analytics,* I, Chapters 2, 10-11, 19; II, Chapter 11. *Sophistical Refutations,* Chapter 6. C. Bittle, O.F.M. Cap., *The Domain of Being,* Chapter 5. R. Garrigou-Lagrange, O.P., *Reality,* Chapters 4, 56. G. H. Joyce, S.J., *Principles of Logic,* Chapter 4. F. Sheen, *God and Intelligence,* 146-72. V. E. Smith, *Idea-Men of Today,* 377-89
33 *On Interpretation,* Chapters 7, 9
35 R. Garrigou-Lagrange, O.P., *God: His Existence and His Nature,* I, 181-91. J. F. McCormick, S.J., *Scholastic Metaphysics,* 140-41. J. F. McCormick, S.J., *Natural Theology,* 45-47, 234. *Summa Theologiae,* I, 2-2, 3 (third and fourth ways); I, 84; here the principle is recognized, but not named.

36 *Summa Theologiae,* I, 5-2; I, 16-3
37 G. Phelan, *St. Thomas and Analogy.* H. Renard, S.J., *Philosophy of Being* (second edition), 92-104. *Truth,* 2-11; 2-3, *ad* 3, 4
41 *Summa Theologiae,* I, 3-4 (second reason); I, 4-1 *ad* 3
44 *Summa Theologiae,* I, 16-4

Exercise 2
Some uses of the principle of sufficient reason

A Relationships of the broad principle of sufficient reason to more particular principles.
Directions: State the connection of ideas between the principle of sufficient reason and the other principle named. The key is on pages 137-38.

  1 the principle of causality, 86
  2 the principle of proportionate causality, 87
  3 the principle of finality, 127
  4 the principle of specification by formal object, 178
  5 the principle of hylemorphism, 255
  6 the intelligibility of reality, 527 and 369
  7 the limitation of act by potency, 14
  8 the unlimited nature of pure act, 14 and Thomistic theses 2-3
  9 the inadequacy of an infinite series to explain something superior, 163

B Give the ultimate sufficient reason for each of the following items, as explained and proved in scholastic philosophy. Some items may be answered from several points of view.

The ultimate sufficient reason for:
  1 the beginning of a new being
  2 the existence of this contingent universe
  3 variety in the universe
  4 order in the universe
  5 evil in the universe
  6 the continuing existence of accidents
  7 the life in man
  8 the unity of man's nature
  9 immortality of the human soul
  10 sure discernment of true from false
  11 ontological truth of things
  12 the existence of the natural moral law
  13 the existence of natural rights
  14 the sacredness of natural rights
  15 the limited authority of the state

4
Cause in general

45 Cause and effect are really distinct. *confer* 84c
The principle is true:
A of agent and patient
B of model and copies
C of matter and form as distinct from the whole, their term
D of end to be obtained and end attained

46 Cause as causing and effect as originating or as depending are simultaneous in being.
VARIANT A cause must be (actual) when it is causing.
NOTE The principle is true:
A of efficient cause
B of material and formal causes
C of final cause
D of idea at least as exemplary cause
INFERENCE Present existence of a cause is proved from its present influence, rather than from the present existence of the result.

47 *Dependence of caused on the cause*: When the cause ceases to act or to be, the effect ceases to be insofar as it is dependent on the influence of that cause.
NOTE This is true of all causes.
VARIANTS A Cessante causa, cessat effectus. B Take away the cause, and you take away the effect. But when one takes away the effect, the cause may remain. C Sublata causa, tollitur effectus.

48 The origin or change of a natural body requires the combined influence of end, agent, matter, and form. *confer* 49, 51, 54, 60, 62
VARIANT Everything that is changed is made for something, from something potential, by something actual, and into something.

45-48 REFERENCES
47 *Summa Theologiae,* I, 2-3 (second way); I, 104-1; *Truth,* 5-8 *ad* 8
48 *Metaphysics,* VII, Chapters 7-8; VIII, Chapter 4

5

Change

The changeable (49-50)

49 Only a being having passive potency can undergo true change.
COROLLARY Only a finite being (mixed act) is changeable.
confer 18

50 Every changeable being is a real composite of potency and act as its intrinsic principles. *confer* 17

The source of change (51-53)

51 *The principle of motion*: Whatever is undergoing real change is being changed by another being in act. *confer* 5, 8
VARIANT Self-motion (by the imperfect) is impossible.
NOTE There is also a way of interpreting this principle as applicable to the agent needing a motive. *confer* 127

52 The mover and moved are really distinct from each other and simultaneous in being. *confer* 45-46

53 Every movement arises ultimately from an immovable agent or end.

Term of change (54-56)

54 Every change needs a good as object moving the agent. Therefore, the end is also a mover. *confer* 127

55 Becoming is for the sake of being.

56 Change is specified by and named from its term. Thus, it is called substantial, qualitative, intentional, physical, or spiritual change, and so on. *confer* 452

Substantial change—generation and corruption (57-62)

57 In natural or physical change the generation of one thing is the corruption of the other (through loss or privation of a previous form).
NOTE This is not true of creation nor of intentional or cognitive change.

58 Generation and corruption are from contraries and into contraries.

59 The term of generation (what is generated) is the composite, not the form alone nor the matter.

VARIANT Forma non fit.

60 Form is the end of generation. *confer* 175

VARIANT The end of generation is a likeness of the form of the generating agent. *confer* 95, 358

NOTE 57-60 may be summed up in the dictum: The principles of a natural body are matter, form, and privation.

61 Material change is always in time and in place.

62 The origin or change of a natural body requires the combined influence of end, agent, matter, and form. *confer* 48

VARIANT Everything that changes is something potential and is changed by some actual being into something for the sake of something or some one.

49-62 REFERENCES

General references: *Physics,* II, Chapters 1, 7; III, Chapters 1-3; VII, Chapters 1-2. *On Generation and Corruption,* I, Chapter 3; II, Chapters 3, 9. *Metaphysics,* VII, Chapters 7-9; XI, Chapter 6, 1063a 20 for 62. J. A. McWilliams, S.J., *Physics and Philosophy: A Study of Saint Thomas's Commentary on the Eight Books of Aristotle's Physics.* V. E. Smith, *Philosophical Physics*

59 *Summa Theologiae,* I, 65-4

6

Conscience

NOTE The principles refer to antecedent conscience.

63 A prudently certain conscience, whether correct or invincibly erroneous, must be obeyed. *confer* 241

64 A vincibly erroneous conscience must be corrected before acting. *confer* 242

65 A prudently certain conscience is (1) sufficient and (2) necessary for moral action.

COROLLARY In a practical doubt, one may not act until the practical doubt is solved directly or reflexly.

Reflex solutions (66-67)

66 In a remaining doubt of conscience (after attempted direct solution), when the doubt concerns the certain right of another or an end necessarily to be attained, the safer course must be chosen. In other words, no unnecessary risk of harming oneself or others may be taken.

67 *Principle of probabilism*: In doubt of law, any solidly probable opinion may be followed in acting, since a doubtful law does not bind.

Note that the principle applies both to natural and positive laws, and to their existence, meaning, extent of obligation, or applicability to the present case. It does not apply to the doubt of validity of a certainly existing, clear, and applicable positive law.

NOTE Some secondary rules on certainty and doubt, that are occasionally called reflex principles, are given to box in the areas in which the principles of the safer course and of probability apply, as well as to indicate better what doubts are to be taken seriously.

A In doubt, one may judge of an act according to what usually happens or what one habitually does.

B In doubt, one may act as prudent good people ordinarily do or as approved authorities on the subject allow.

c In a remaining doubt of the extent or degree of obligation of a law, only the minimum certain obligation is to be exacted.

D In doubt of guilt or authorship of a fact, every one is to be presumed innocent until there is proof of the fact of his guilt. *confer* 291

E Hence, unfounded suspicions and punitive measures before proof of guilt violate the safer course against some one's certain right. *confer* 66

F In doubt about the occurrence of a fact, the fact is not to be presumed but must be proved. *confer* 291

G In doubt about the validity of an act that has been performed, the act is to be presumed to be valid until there is proof of its invalidity.

In some acts certainty is required, as in acts necessary by a necessity of means, such as baptism, and in acts needed to safeguard others' rights. Here the doubt must be resolved by conditional repetition of the required act. *confer* 66

H In doubt about the validity of a positive law, the law is presumed to be valid for the sake of the common good and to preserve the certain right of authority.

I In an unsolved doubt concerning a right or title, the present possessor's right is preferred to the doubtful (unproved) right of other claimants. This is especially true (1) of some one who gained possession in good faith, or (2) of some one who used proper contractual formalities when he gained possession in doubtful faith.

68 Even a valid positive law is not binding in conscience in particular instances when its observance entails difficulties disproportionate to the importance and purpose of the law. *confer* 337c, 2

63-68 REFERENCES

General references: T. J. Higgins, S.J., *Man as Man*, Chapter 8. *Summa Theologiae*, I-II, 19-6. *Truth*, 17-3, 4, 5. Also standard works on moral theology such as E. Healy, S.J., *Moral Guidance*, and H. Davis, S.J., *Moral and Pastoral Theology*, Volume I

Exercise 3
Principles concerning conscience

Directions: A Make a clear, fair estimate of the factual situation. B Consider what principles on conscience are relevant to the situation. C State your view of the right or wrong of the matter. The key is on pages 138-39.

1 A child asks his father whether he may play with a ouija board. The parent does not know whether it is good or not, but tells the child to do as he pleases.

2 An instructor is highly suspicious that one of his students copied in an examination, but he is not certain. May he assign a failing grade to the suspected paper on the presumption of copying?

3 A young American is in love with a fervent communist miss. He wonders whether he is morally safe in proposing to marry her.

4 A policeman reports an auto license number as that of a car involved in a hit-and-run accident. But the policeman knows that his glasses need refitting and that he may have misread one number of the reported license plate.

5 A pharmacist is filling out a legitimate prescription for sleeping pills. But he notices that the customer is depressed and begins to wonder

whether there is danger of an overdose. He warns the customer but does not withhold the prescription nor notify the customer's physician about his suspicions.

6 A city official is unsure whether a certain type of business is required to pay for an occupational license. But in order to get revenue he assesses the license tax with all due formalities.

7 A juror in a murder case is not satisfied of either the guilt or the innocence of the accused. The other jurors have all voted for guilt. What may or must the unconvinced juror do?

8 A politician, hungry for popularity, repeats immodest stories which he has picked up, arguing that probably they will do harm to nobody. He does not judge the stories to be any worse than those people hear in plays or over television and to which they have been accustomed.

9 A young man appeals to a doctor for a recommendation to a medical school. The doctor does not know enough about the applicant to give an opinion to the admissions committee of the medical school. What may he do?

10 A student told her teacher: "Don't tell me arguments against birth control. I do not want to know them. I do not want babies when I am married."

11 Late for duty, the nurse put on gloves that certainly were not sterilized. But she argued that it was necessary to start work at once and there was little probability that the gloves were infectious or contaminated.

12 An earnest and God-fearing Jew has serious doubts whether his Hebrew religion is the will of God. What must he do to settle his doubt?

13 A Catholic mother intends to send her daughter of high-school age to a fashionable school without inquiry into the content of teaching, the moral atmosphere, and the religious opportunities available at that school.

14 A college man and his girl buy tickets for a movie that is widely mentioned as objectionable. They argue that the criticisms of this particular movie are highly exaggerated.

7

Definitions

69 *Rule of correctness*: A correct definition must be (1) clear, (2) reciprocal, (3) positive when possible, and (4) stated in terms different from the term to be defined.

NOTE Clearness ordinarily requires that the definition be brief, not unusual in language, not metaphorical, and stated in better known terms.

70 *Method in defining*:

A Individuals are not defined, but described and identified.

B The self-evident is not defined.

C An object of immediate experience usually cannot be defined by anything simpler than itself.

D The transcendentals and the primary divisions of being cannot receive essential definitions.

E Relatives are defined by their correlatives. *confer* 477

COROLLARY Hence, habits, dispositions, and acts are defined by their formal objects. Potencies are defined by their corresponding acts.

71 An essential definition is one, constant, immutable, necessary, eternal, and indivisible.

NOTE The same properties belong to abstracted essences or to the "ideas."

72 *Rule on truth of definitions*:

A Nominal definitions must be tested by historical origins of words or by their use in the special source which has arbitrarily defined them in a given framework of reference.

B Real definitions depend on the objective validity of the induction on which they are based.

C Definitions of natural bodies must include both matter and form. *confer* 167-68, 416

69-72 REFERENCES

General references: *Topics,* VI; VII, Chapter 3. *Posterior Analytics,* II, Chapters 10, 13. G. H. Joyce, S.J., *Principles of Logic,* Chapter 10. V. E. Smith, "Definitions," in *From an Abundant Spring* (edited by *Thomist* editors), 337-62. *On Being and Essence,* Chapters 2, 6

8
Distinctions

73 Union is opposed to separation but not to distinction among united parts or principles or constituents of a being.

74 Wherever there is a union of the distinct, there is composite being.

75 The distinction, plurality, variety, and inequality of finite things originate from A the infinite goodness of God which is imitable only in many different species; B the wisdom of God setting order and its degrees among things; and c the choice of God to manifest His goodness in multiple ways. *confer* 189, 216-18

76 Substantial form is the intrinsic principle of differences between species. Accidental forms are the intrinsic principles of differences, varieties, and inequalities within the same species. *confer* 171-72
NOTE Since the end serves as the form in moral matters, human acts are differentiated by their ends, and societies are specified by their ends. *confer* 129

77 Signate matter is the ultimate principle of individuation or of numerical distinction between natural bodies in the same species.
COROLLARY An incorporeal complete finite being is numerically as well as specifically distinguished by its form. *confer* Thomistic thesis 11

78 *Principle of identity and difference,* ontological formula: Things or objective concepts which are the same as a third thing or objective concept are the same as each other. But if one of them is the same as a third and the other is different from that same third, these two are different from each other.
NOTE This principle is especially applicable to specific and moral identities and differences.
Principle of identity and difference, logical formula: We ought to affirm as true the mutual identity of two things (natures or objective concepts) which are the same as a third thing (nature or objective concept) with which they are compared; we ought to deny their identity if one is the same as the third and the other is different from this same third.

79 Distinctions between beings and constituents of beings are not to be multiplied without good reason.

NOTE This is an application of the principle of economy, 292, to the question of real distinctions.

COROLLARY Hence, essential or real distinction is not to be affirmed without a clear sign.

80 Things are essentially distinct if one of them has one or more types of operations which the other totally lacks or if one is the analogical cause of the other. *confer* 163, corollary

81 One being or perfection is essentially superior to another if it has one or more attributes or operations which are totally different and totally better than those of another being, or which are free from all the limitations found in the lower nature.

The following formula of identification of essential superiority in natural bodies may be used: Perfection A in a being excels B when A implies B's presence, but not vice versa.

NOTE Natures lacking this criterion may be A only numerically distinct, or B merely different in degree, or C simply disparate in essence.

82 The powers of a finite being are multiplied according to the completely diverse formal objects with which they deal. *confer* 178-79

83 Operative habits are distinguished generically by the powers which they perfect, and specifically by the formal objects of their operations. *confer* 207

84 The criteria or norms of real distinction between wholes or between principles and parts of the same whole:

A Whatever is really separate or really separable from another is really distinct from that other.

B Whatever are accidentally united are distinct and usually separable.

C Whatever has properties and attributes that are contradictory or contrary to the properties of another being or principle of the same being is really distinct from that other being or principle. *confer* 34, 78

D An agent is really distinct from its effect(s). See 45, but also note 28 on action and passion. Also see an application in Thomistic thesis 6.

E Powers, habits, and acts are really distinguished by their diverse formal objects. *confer* 82-83, 178

F Whatever is essentially distinct from another is also really distinct from that other, since each is a whole with its own form. *confer* 76, 164-65

G Principles of being related to each other as act and potency, whether in the same order of being or in different orders of being within the same whole, are really distinct from each other. *confer* 13

H Natures or attributes represented by *adequately* distinct objective concepts are really distinct from each other.

NOTE This criterion assumes that the concepts have been objectively derived from things. Hence, it is not a mere movement from a mental to a real distinction.

I A real attribute indirectly or obliquely predicated of a real subject is really distinct from that subject.

NOTE Oblique predication does not say what the being is, but states what it has, how it operates, or what are its relations, passions, and accidents.

73-84 REFERENCES

75 *Summa Theologiae,* I, 47

77 *On Being and Essence,* Chapter 4

78 *Summa Theologiae,* I, 28-3 ad 1

79 For Ockham's use of this principle in regard to real distinctions, see F. Copleston, S.J., *History of Philosophy,* III, Index, "Economy, principle of."

80-81 Boethius, *Consolation of Philosophy,* V, prose 4. *Truth,* 15-1 ad 2

84 J. F. McCormick, S.J., *Scholastic Metaphysics,* 75, 105-06, 117, 142. H. Renard, S.J., *Philosophy of Being* (second edition), 39-45, 57-61, 70-74. *Summa Theologiae,* I, 77-1; I-II, 54 (especially 2). *Contra Gentiles,* I, Chapter 13; IV, Chapter 24. *Truth,* 15-2. C. Vollert, S.J. (translator and editor), *Francis Suarez "On the Various Kinds of Distinctions,"* especially Section II

Exercise 4

Identifying essential superiority

Directions: Give reasons why the being or type of being mentioned in item A is essentially superior to the being or type of being in item B. The reasons will be operations or characteristics in A which are superior and totally lacking in B. The key is on page 139.

Example: God A is essentially superior to any creature B for He *alone* is uncaused, necessary in existence, infinite, Creator of being. Uncaused, necessary, infinite being is free of limitations and dependence of any kind; power to create is completely independent, unrestricted, free causal power.

Problems

1 A living body A is essentially superior to a nonliving body B.
2 A animal   B a plant
3 A plant   B inanimate things
4 A thought   B sensation
5 A will   B sensitive appetites
6 A men   B brute animals
7 A human soul   B matter of the human body
8 A angelic spirit   B human soul
   Theological example
9 A soul in sanctifying B soul without grace
   grace

Give reasons for essential equality or lack of essential superiority.

10 A tree is not essentially superior to a blade of grass.
11 One human being has no *natural* superiority to any other human being. (Accidental differences and superiority are granted.)

Exercise 5
Identifying real distinctions by use of criteria

Directions: The criteria for real distinctions in 84 serve as majors for proof of the presence of real distinctions. The following exercise will help to gain familiarity with the criteria and with their use in philosophy. The pertinent criteria are given for the problem. It is advised that they be written out and the minor needed for each argument given. The key is on page 139.

Example: God is really distinct from the world.
A Major.   The efficient cause is really distinct from its effects. (84D)
  Minor.   But God is the efficient cause of the world.
  Therefore, God is really distinct from the world.
B Beings with opposite attributes are really distinct from each other. (84c)
  But God is necessary, subsistent, infinite, eternal, pure act, and so on; the world is contingent, dependent, finite, temporal, mixed with potency, and so on.
  Therefore, God is really distinct from the world.
c What is really superior to another is really distinct from the other. (84F)
  But God is essentially superior to the world. (See example in Exercise 4.)
  Therefore, God is really distinct from the world.

1 Use criteria A, C, G, and H to show the real distinction of the human soul from the matter of the body in the human being.

2 Use criteria C and G to show the real distinction of the human soul from the human intellect.

3 Use criteria C and E to show the real distinction of the human intellect from the power of vision.

4 Use criterion E to show the real distinction of the intellect from the will.

5 Use criteria A, B, D, and G to show the real distinction of the intellect from one of its acts of reasoning.

6 Use criteria C, G, and H to show the real distinction of finite essence from the act of finite existence in the same being.

7 Use criteria A, G, and H to show the real distinction of matter and substantial form.

9

Division

85 Rules on correctness in logical division:

A The division must be complete so that all the members of the division together equal the whole class divided.

NOTE The completeness must be sufficient for the purpose in view.

B No member may exceed or equal the whole class of which it is only a member.

C No member may include another member. That is, the members must be opposites.

D The division must be orderly. Hence, it must proceed from one constant basis or principle; and any needed subdivisions must be the immediate members of the higher class.

85 REFERENCES

G. H. Joyce, S.J., *Principles of Logic,* Chapters 10, 24

10

Efficient causality

86 *The principle of causality* (that is, of efficient causality or agency): Every contingent being requires an efficient cause for its existence, continuance in existence, and any real changes occurring in it; and this cause is really distinct from the contingent being.

VARIANTS Some of these express only part of the truth of the principle. A No being can produce itself. B No potency can actualize itself, but can be brought to actuality only by a distinct being in act. *confer* 5 C Nothing comes from nothing; being comes only from being. D Whatever begins to exist requires an efficient cause of its existence. E Every physical change requires a cause distinct from the subject changed and the new form arising in the subject. *confer* 51 F Whatever comes to be comes to be from another being. G Every new being requires an efficient cause of its existence.

Signs of contingency of a being are:

A beginning to be, previous nonexistence

B any intrinsic change, any acquisition or loss of either substantial or accidental form

C real dependence on another

D participation, multiplicity, membership in a genus or species

E imperfection, incompleteness, any passive potency, materiality, composition

The principle of proportionate causality (87-94)

87 A Stated from the viewpoint of the effect: The effect cannot be better than the cause(s) producing it.

B Stated from the viewpoint of the cause: The cause must possess, at least virtually but not necessarily formally, whatever perfection it gives to the effect.

C Stated from the viewpoint of the active principle in the cause: Every agent acts according to its form. *confer* 95, 174, 176, 422

VARIANT Every agent acts according to its nature in act.

D Stated from the viewpoint of the activities as proceeding from the cause: Activities cannot surpass the perfection of the natures, forms, and powers which perform them. *confer* 99

88 The lower nature cannot do something "proper" to a higher nature except with the aid of the higher nature.

89 The First Cause can produce by Himself alone whatever He produces with secondary causes or whatever He gives to secondary causes the power to do.

90 Nothing acts upon its equal in perfection. *confer* 104D, 364

91 No being by itself alone can produce its equal in perfection.

92 The cause always surpasses the effect somehow.
VARIANTS A The cause is nobler than the effect. B Propter quod unumquodque tale, et illud magis. That is, the cause of anything is that kind of thing in a greater degree.

93 When the power of the mover exceeds the whole capacity of the moved, the moved is necessarily subject to that power.

94 The greater or more universal the effect, the more powerful and excellent is its cause.

The principle of resemblance of cause and its effects (95-96)

95 A Every agent produces a thing that is in some degree like its own form. (This is sometimes called *the principle of proper causality. confer* 60, variant; 87c; 358)
VARIANT Like begets its own like.
APPLICATIONS (1) Every habit comes from like or proper acts. *confer* 205, 362 (2) Substance can come only from substance. (3) All life comes from life. (Pasteur's law, *confer* 360) (4) Every cell from a cell.
B Agents that act through knowledge make things like their ideas (or their operations), but not always univocally like their own natures. *confer* 351
C Both an instrumental cause and a subordinate cause make the effect like to the form and intention of the principal cause on which it depends.

96 Every effect has at least an analogical likeness to the form and intention of its (principal) cause. Likewise, it bears some trace of the influence of the instrumental cause.

Agere sequitur esse. Activity follows existence (97-102)

97 Activity follows existence. Agere sequitur esse. Some of the many variants follow.
VARIANTS A Operari sequitur naturam vel formam. B Operatio sequitur essentiam. C As a thing acts, so it is. D As a thing is,

so it acts. E The measure and kind of operation expresses the mode of being of a nature. F The mode of being determines the mode of operation. G Actions reveal the essence. H Each thing acts according to its own form. *confer* 87c
This serviceable principle occurs in five interrelated meanings and uses (98-102).

98 *Priority* of being: A thing must be before it can cause.
VARIANTS A A thing cannot act unless or until it is. B Actuality and power are prerequisite to the exercise of causality or any real change or newness of being.

99 *Proportion*: Activities cannot surpass the perfection of the being (nature, form, power) which is the principle from which these proceed. *confer* 87D

100 *Resemblance*: The acts are like the nature. *confer* 95

101 *Possession*: The acts belong to the being, and so are predicated of the suppositum. *confer* 454

102 *Knowledge of cause through the acts*: The acts reveal the existence of the cause; and especially the characteristic and immanent acts reveal the nature of the cause which produces them. *confer* 108

Requirements for causal action (103-06)

103 Every agent when sufficiently in act according to its natural due capacities tends to its own proper activity.

104 For the exercise of causality, there must be:
A a really existing cause *confer* 98
B adequate and proximate power in the cause *confer* 87
C presence of the cause and contact, immediate or mediate, with the patient (that is, no obstacles, unimpeded action)
D real distinction, inequality, and formal dissimilarity at the start of action between the cause and patient *confer* 45, 58, 90
E proximate passive potency in the patient for the perfection to be caused (but for creating mere possibility suffices)
F God's concurrence with any created activity

105 The agent as agent does not change nor gain nor lose any perfection when acting. *confer* 29

106 Every complete substance can be an agent.
VARIANT All finite beings attain their end by operation and in operation. *confer* 511

107 *The principle of uniformity of nature*: A necessary or natural cause always produces the same effect, one effect, and always acts with the same intensity and in the same manner.

VARIANT The same natural (necessary) causes under the same adequate set of circumstances always produce the same result(s). *confer* 111, 423

A posteriori knowledge of causes (108-12)

108 Every effect when known can lead to some knowledge of the existence, power, and nature of its cause. The knowledge gained may however be only analogical because of the unlikeness between the effect and the cause in some respects. *confer* 102, 327-30, 436

109 The existence of a cause is known from its *present* influence on the effect. *confer* 296

110 Among complex antecedents of an event, the cause of the phenomenon is that factor in whose presence the phenomenon occurs, in whose absence it does not occur, and in whose variation of strength the phenomenon varies in strength.

111 The activity and effects of a natural (necessary) cause are predictable in advance, given both presence of the cause and the same circumstances and knowledge of that presence of cause and circumstances. *confer* 107

112 Contrary effects have contrary causes, while a uniform constant effect needs a uniform and constant cause.

Multiple causes (113-18)

113 The causality of the first cause and of second causes is intrinsically analogous both in the mode of causal action and in the term of action. *confer* 88-89

114 Two agents may be causes of diverse perfections in each other by mutual interaction.

VARIANT Causae ad invicem sunt causae.

115 The instrumental cause acts only as moved, used, or controlled by the principal. It "intends" the effect of the principal cause. It limits and particularizes the principal's action. *confer* 97

116 The cause of a cause is also the cause of the thing caused by that (the secondary, dependent) cause. (Causa causae est causa causati.)

This principle implies that the two or more causes are acting simultaneously. Then it is true:

A of a series or set of essentially subordinate causes

B of God's immediate physical concurrence to the physical entity of any causal operation and effect

C of the intended and foreseen moral cooperation of all free causes

NOTE TO A Hence, the metaphysical value of the dictum of law is clear: What one does through another, one does by one's self. (Qui facit per alium facit per se.)

117 Immanent action, however aided by external agents, always has the living agent itself as its principal cause.

118 End and agent complement each other's causality. *confer* 62

Priority (119-21)

119 The cause as being has priority of nature and excellence to the being of the effect. Often there is also priority of time.

120 A universal and nonunivocal cause is prior to a particular and univocal cause.

121 The effect is often prior in our knowledge and leads to a knowledge of its cause. *confer* 108, 450-51

NOTE See also 45 (distinction of cause and effect), 46 (simultaneity), and 47 (degree of dependence).

86-121 REFERENCES

86 J. F. McCormick, S.J., *Scholastic Metaphysics*, Chapter 9. J. F. McCormick, S.J., *Natural Theology*, Chapters 4, 11. F. X. Meehan, *Efficient Causality in Aristotle and St. Thomas*, Chapters 6, 12. *On Being and Essence*, Chapter 4. *Summa Theologiae*, I, 3-4 (first argument); I, 44-1. *Contra Gentiles*, II, Chapter 1; III, Chapters 69 (replies), 97. *On the Power of God*, 3-5; 3-8

87 *Scholastic Metaphysics*, 154-55, 210-11. *Natural Theology*, 21, 54, 107, 256-57, 271. *Efficient Causality in Aristotle and St. Thomas*, 228-35. *Summa Theologiae*, I, 19-4 (third argument); I, 44-2 (objection 3 and reply to 3); I-II, 63-3. *Contra Gentiles*, II, Chapter 21 (especially the third argument); III, Chapter 52

92 *Posterior Analytics*, I, Chapter 2. *Truth*, 7-8 *ad* 1

93 *Summa Theologiae*, I, 82-2

95-96 *Metaphysics*, VII, Chapter 9 (near end on substance). *Summa Theologiae*, I, 4-2, 3, 7 *ad* 1; I, 6-1; I, 19-4 (third argument); I, 25-2 *ad* 2; I, 45-5 (paragraphs 2 and 3); I-II, 112-1 *ad* 1, 2. *Contra Gentiles*, II, Chapter 46 (especially arguments 4 and 5); III, Chapters 19 (arguments 2 and 4), 51; IV, Chapter 7 (fifth last paragraph). *On the Power of God*, 7-1 *ad* 8, 2. *Truth*, 5-8 *ad* 8; 26-7 on four modes of resemblance of effect to cause

97-102 *Scholastic Metaphysics,* 44-45, 154-56, 215. *Summa Theologiae,* very often, for example, I, 29-1 *ad* 3; I, 45-5 *ad* 3; I, 75-2 (near end of corpus); I, 76-1 (paragraph 6); I, 115-1. On correct wording of the principle, see J. Anderson, *The Cause of Being,* 1, footnote.

104 *Metaphysics,* IX, Chapter 7. *Efficient Causality in Aristotle and St. Thomas,* 67-72, 235-38, 272 ff.

105 *Summa Theologiae,* I-II, 51-2 *ad* 1

106 *Efficient Causality in Aristotle and St. Thomas,* 308-17 (and *passim* in the same chapter); also in Chapter IX, Section V, 2. *Contra Gentiles,* III, Chapters 68-70

107 *On Generation and Corruption,* II, Chapter 10. G. H. Joyce, S.J., *Principles of Logic,* Chapter 15. *Efficient Causality in Aristotle and St. Thomas,* Chapters 7, 13. *Natural Theology,* 255-58. *Summa Theologiae,* I, 19-4 (second way); I, 47-1 *ad* 1

108 *Summa Theologiae,* I, 2-2; I, 29-1 *ad* 3; I, 45-5 *ad* 3; I, 62-1. *Contra Gentiles,* III, Chapter 49

109 *Posterior Analytics,* II, Chapters 12, 16

110 *Principles of Logic,* Chapter 20

112 *On Generation and Corruption,* II, Chapter 10

114 *Summa Theologiae,* I, 82-4 *ad* 1

115 G. Smith, S.J., *Natural Theology,* 92-95. *Summa Theologiae,* III, 62-1, 4. *Contra Gentiles,* II, Chapter 21. *On the Power of God,* 3-4

120 *Summa Theologiae,* I, 13-5 *ad* 1

Exercise 6
Citation of principles on efficient causality

A Complete. The key is on page 140.

1 A cause is . . . distinct from its effect.
2 Effects can lead us to the . . . of . . . , . . . , and . . . of causes.
3 A being . . . actualize a being equal to . . . in perfection.
4 Prediction of action of . . . causes is possible to one with sufficient knowledge.
5 God needs . . . . . . cause to help Him.
6 The creature always needs . . . , ... , to help it.
7 The . . . . . . cause of immanent acts always is the . . . being.

B State in full.

1 the principle of causality
2 the principle of proportionate causality (any point of view of it)
3 the principle of uniform causality
4 the marks of a contingent being
5 the five aspects of the maxim: "Activity follows existence."
6 the set of requirements for causality

C Revise these incorrect citations by (1) canceling wrong words or order, *and* (2) writing the correct and true citation or *addition* to the statement.

    1 Every effect has a cause.
    2 The effect is very similar to the instrumental cause.
    3 When the effect ceases, the cause ceases to be.
    4 A cause as cause is prior to the effect.
    5 A cause must contain its effect materially and formally.
    6 Every result completely reveals the nature of its cause.
    7 Knowledge of efficient causes eliminates the need for final causes.
    8 When the cause ceases to act, the effect ceases to be.

Exercise 7
Action follows existence

Directions: Write down principle 102 and its several connoted meanings. Then study the frequent use of the principle in the philosophy of man or rational psychology. State what acts are performed by living beings, and in particular by men, that show each conclusion. The key is on pages 140-41.

Example: What acts show that I am a cause? REPLY: A cause is a being which by its activity produces something. A man knows that he is the cause of his efforts, as to rise in the morning, to lift heavy objects, to direct his attention to a task and away from distractions, to control his feelings, to change objects outside him as in throwing a baseball, or digging a hole, or tearing a piece of paper.

Problems
    1 What acts show life in a being?
    2 What acts show existence of instincts in animals?
    3 What acts show the unity of man?
    4 What acts show the spirituality of the human intellect?
    5 What acts show that in sensation there is a material intrinsic constituent?
    6 What acts show the existence of habits in man?
    7 What acts show the spirituality of the human soul?
    8 What acts show the simplicity of the human soul?
    9 What acts show the soul's intrinsic independence of the body?
  10 What acts show the soul's extrinsic dependence on the body?
  11 What acts show some freedom of the rational appetite or will?
  12 What acts show the occurrence of accidental changes in man?
  13 What acts show that man acts with conscious purposes?
  14 What acts show the permanence of the self?
  15 What acts can show human abilities: for example, intellectual abilities or I.Q., mechanical abilities, health or illness, good or bad character, social leadership, athletic abilities, civic loyalty?

Exercise 8
Uses of principles on efficient causality

Directions: Write out the full statement, not merely the name, of the principle which most closely pertains to the application presented. The key is on page 141.

Example: Stop the trouble at its source. PRINCIPLE: When the cause ceases to act, the effect ceases in as far as it depended on that cause.

1 As we sow, so we reap. (There may be two principles involved here.)
2 Lunar eclipses can be predicted centuries in advance of their happening.
3 No success without effort.
4 Effects are a picture book of their makers.
5 His fingerprints betrayed the bandit.
6 A self-originating universe is impossible.
7 That student's conduct shows that he has had fine home training.
8 "Only God can make a tree."
9 God, not nature, heals in miraculous cures. (Two principles are involved in this one.)
10 An ounce of prevention is worth a pound of cure.
11 His alibi was perfect; so, he could not have been the murderer.
12 Shakespeare reveals himself in his plays.
13 Material things can produce no spiritual effects in our souls.
14 He talks like a communist; he acts like a communist; he associates with communists. So, I say that he is a communist.
15 While this drug will soothe your pain, only extraction of that tooth will cure you.
16 A farmer does not have to be a big potato to raise potatoes.
17 We can be quite sure that the horse pulls the wagon and not the wagon pushes the horse. (Two principles at least are involved.)
18 By their fruits you shall know them—as good men or bad men.
19 The civilization of the Egyptians is well understood from the relics in the pyramid tombs.
20 His conversation betrays the educated man; his manners betray the gentleman; his careful opinions betray the judicious man.

11
End—final cause

122 The end is the cause of all causes.
VARIANT The end is the first of the causes.

123 The end is the first in the order of intention, the last in the order of achievement or execution.
VARIANT That which is last in the order of achievement is first in the order of ends.

124 The ultimate end is the end of all other ends.
VARIANTS A The supreme good is the supreme end. B The ultimate end is the first of all causes.

125 The end (that is, the good) is the first principle in the practical order.

126 The end is prior to the means in excellence and in the order of intention.

127 *Principle of finality*: Every agent or nature in acting must act for an end.
VARIANTS A Every being seeks its own perfection. B Every agent acts for a good. C Every nature is ordered to an end. D Nature does nothing in vain. *confer* 432 E No agent intends evil as such. *confer* 187 F The end is the first principle of activity. *confer* 125 G The end is the reason for all movement and progress. H Nothing can be done except with some end in view. I Absolute chance is impossible.

128 There must be an ultimate (supreme, first) final cause of the universe.

129 The specific or particular end or good determines and specifies the particular type of nature and of its powers.
COROLLARIES A The end specifies a society. *confer* 76 B The end specifies and often gives its name to a change. *confer* 56

130 Its end is the formal object of any appetitive and of any active power.

131 Specific natures determine or define intrinsic ends.

132 A nature, its powers, its characteristic or specific activities, its intrinsic end or ends, and the formal objects of its powers are proportionate to each other. *confer 87, 420*
VARIANT Such as a thing is, such is its operation, and such is the end to which it tends.

133 The order of ends and the order of appetites (agents) correspond. (Thus, the highest end is the object of the highest appetite attained in its best operation.) *confer 226*

Relation of ends and means (134-38)

134 The end is the principle and measure of the means. See 198 and 384 for detailed applications.
COROLLARIES A The end is the correct principle of the selection, direction, order (arrangement), and subordination of the means. B The end is the principle of unity in the parts of a process. C The end is the measure of the suitability, unsuitability, timeliness, and sufficiency of the means. D The end should dominate and control the means and all merely useful goods.

135 The means precede the end in the order of execution.

136 When the end ceases, the sufficient reason for the means ceases. *confer 47*

137 He who seriously wills the end wills the necessary means to the end.
COROLLARY Hence, the author of nature seriously wills the natural essential means for natural purposes. *confer 565*

138 The imperfect exists for the sake of the perfect, matter for form, powers for their operations, and parts for the whole. *confer 8, 198, 547*

Manner of knowing and willing ends (139-41)

139 Finality and order both in plan and in execution presuppose and indicate the activity of some intellectual agent.

140 Agents acting for ends manifest finality in analogical ways. A God knows and wills the end, without being caused by the end to will it. B Intellectual creatures, angels and men, in their fully intellectual and voluntary operations, formally intend ends; and these cause their activity. C Nonintellectual creatures are directed to ends by the necessity of their natures and the laws of their being, even without their own foreknowledge and intention of the end. They act as instruments of their authors, especially of the Author of nature.

141 The excellence of ends attained, the organization of means, the complex unity of plan and process, and the permanent quality of results are a sign of proportionately high intelligence in the principal agent.

NOTE   Compare with principle of proportionate causality, 87.

Discovery of intrinsic natural ends (142-45)

142 The end of the universe can be known a priori from the perfection of the infinite will of God.

143 The specific natural intrinsic purpose of a created nature cannot be learned a priori, but only a posteriori. The intrinsic natural purpose of a nature is learned by study of the type of goods of which its powers are capable, the type of goods for which it shows constant and universal tendencies, and the type of goods for which it has constant and common needs. These goods and these powers, tendencies, and needs are in turn known from the observed characteristic activities of a nature. *confer* 102, 108, 129, 132

COROLLARY   Variable choice is not a criterion of the intrinsic end of man.

144 In a complex being the end of the supreme faculty or power is the end of the whole being. (Some say: of its highest appetite.)

145 The end of the whole is the end of the parts in as far as they are parts of that whole. *confer* 547

Types of end and some of their relationships (146-54)

146 All natures of the same species have the same intrinsic end. *confer* 359, 428

NOTE   The same degree of perfection of the intrinsic end is not, however, attained by all members of the species.

147 The intrinsic end of a nature is constant and ineradicable as long as the nature remains essentially the same.

148 The intrinsic or natural end is not an object of choice.

149 The attainment of a natural end is frequently conditioned upon choice of right means or upon favorable external circumstances.

150 The ultimate perfection (that is, end) of a power is its operation. VARIANTS A A thing is for the sake of its activity. *confer* 138 B The ultimate intrinsic perfection of a nature is the best operation of its best power on the best object of which the power is capable. *confer* 133 c The operation proper to a thing is its end.

151 Proximate ends do not exclude ultimate ends if they can be related as means to the ultimate end.

152 The end of the agent is the same as the end of the patient. VARIANT The end of the work is always reducible to the end of the agent of that work. APPLICATION What nature intends, God intends. *confer* 429

153 The end of generation is the form of the generated in as far as it is like the form of the generator. VARIANT Every agent intends some likeness of itself. *confer* 95-96

154 *Continuity of ends*: Divine Wisdom always joins the ends of the lower orders of being with the principles of the higher order. *confer* 138, 215

122-54 REFERENCES
General references: *Physics*, II, Chapters 3, 8. *Metaphysics*, II, Chapter 2. *Parts of Animals*, I, Chapter 1. *Nicomachaean Ethics*, I, Chapters 1-2, 7; VII, Chapter 8. R. Garrigou-Lagrange, O.P., *God: His Existence and His Nature*, I, 199-205, 345-72. Brother Benignus Gerrity, F.S.C., *Nature, Knowledge, and God*, Chapter 5. J. B. McAllister, C.S.Sp., "Chance in Aristotle and Aquinas," in J. K. Ryan (editor), *Philosophical Studies in Honor of the Very Reverend Ignatius Smith, O.P.*, 76-91. J. F. McCormick, S.J., *Scholastic Metaphysics*, 156-59, 169-79. J. F. McCormick, S.J., *Natural Theology*, Chapters 5, 12, especially 62-74. *Contra Gentiles*, III, Chapters 2-3, 16-18, 22, 24-25, 112 (sixth paragraph). *Summa Theologiae*, I, 2-3 (fifth way); I, 22-2; I, 44-4; I, 105-5; I-II, 1, 12, 13; I, 90-2; II-II, 47; II-II, 66-1, 2. *On the Power of God*, 1-5. *Truth*, 5-2

134 *Summa Theologiae*, I-II, 95-3; I-II, 96-1; I-II, 101-1 *ad* 1; I-II, 102-1; II-II, 152-2. *Contra Gentiles*, I, Chapter 1

136 *Summa Theologiae*, I-II, 4-4 (objections and reply 3)

138 *Summa Theologiae*, I, 65-2 (second paragraph of corpus). *Contra Gentiles*, I, Chapter 86; III, Chapter 129

139 *Contra Gentiles*, II, Chapter 24 (third argument)

Exercise 9
Citation of principles on end

A Complete. The key is on page 142.

    1 The end is last in . . . , first in . . .
    2 Every being exists for the sake of . . .
    3 Persons alone act . . . for their ends.
    4 When the . . . ceases, the . . . ceases.
    5 Ends measure means in these (five) ways: . . .
    6 Its end . . . the nature.

B State in full.

    1 the principle of finality
    2 the basic principle on the relation of end to means
    3 the principle on discovery of intrinsic natural ends
    4 proportion between natures and ends
    5 the priority of end (several aspects)

C Revise these incorrect citations by (1) canceling wrong words or order, *and* (2) writing in the correct and true citation or *addition* to the statement.

    1 The end of the whole is the sum of the purposes of the parts.
    2 Effective action is the cause of all causes.
    3 Every nature must and will attain its highest intrinsic end.
    4 Every nature must know the end for which it is acting.
    5 The ultimate end is the least of the ends.
    6 The pursuit of proximate ends prevents attainment of the ultimate end.

Exercise 10
Uses of principles on final cause

Directions: Write out the full statement, not merely the name, of the principle which most closely pertains to the application presented. The key is on page 142.

Example: APPLICATION: The orator must present motives for acting. PRINCIPLE: The purpose is the reason for all activity.

    1 A worthy and high aim helps much to integrate one's personality.
    2 "Order is heaven's first law."
    3 The author of the universe has a very superior intelligence.
    4 No success without planning.
    5 "The secret of success is constancy of purpose."—Disraeli
    6 Failures are often condemned by the phrase, "too little and too late."

7 What nature intends, God intends. (See also 429.)

8 The dramatic critic must consider the motivation of plot and characters, and not merely techniques of language and staging.

9 Because there is an eternal law, there must be a natural moral law.

10 The need of the good is the beginning of law.

11 Laws contrary to the common good cannot bind subjects.

12 Man's capacity, tendency, and need for perfect happiness prove that it is his natural purpose in existence.

13 The good of the whole body justifies excision of a seriously diseased part. *confer* 390

14 The human appetite with the highest end is the primary and best appetite of man. (It is the will.)

15 The essential ends of human life and essential duties determine our inalienable natural rights. *confer* 485

16 No good engine has useless parts.

12

Evidence

155 *The principle of evidence*: The objective evidence of being is the criterion of the truth of assent and the motive for certain assent.
VARIANTS A Whatever is objectively evident is true. B The thing in the condition of evidence is the measure of the truth of judgments. *confer* 288, 313

156 A There is no argument against the evidence.
B No inference contrary to the fact(s) is true. *confer* 288-89, 266

157 An explanation or hypothesis must take account of *all* the evidence. *confer* 261

155-57 REFERENCES
Metaphysics, IX, Chapter 10. J. Rickaby, S.J., *The First Principles of Knowledge* (1921 edition), Chapter 13

13
Finite and infinite

158 A Every act that is finite is limited by a potency receiving it.

B Every finite being is a real composite of potency and act as of intrinsic principles of its being.

COROLLARY The basic composition and limitation is that of existence limited by and united with essence. *confer* 18 and Thomistic theses 1-3, 7

159 The substance or substantial form of any finite being is really distinct from its powers; the powers also are really distinct from their operations. *confer* 84, 515, and Thomistic theses 5, 7

160 Every finite being, as possessing potency, is either actually or potentially multiple in its genus or species.

COROLLARY A finite being can be the foundation of a univocal universal concept. *confer* 321

161 The finite is at an unlimited distance from the perfection of the infinite.

162 The infinite and finite being possess no perfection univocally. So, no perfection may be univocally predicated of them both. *confer* 400, 409, and Thomistic thesis 4

163 *Insufficiency of an infinite series*: An infinite series or sum of beings each of which has the same essential nature or characteristic as the one (member of the series) requiring explanation is an insufficient and irrelevant explanation of that nature or characteristic.

COROLLARY In such a series or set of similar natures or characteristics that are not self-explanatory, there cannot be a regress into infinity without a first source of the series that essentially differs from each and all members of the series.

158-63 REFERENCES

158 *Summa Theologiae*, I, 7-1. *Compendium of Theology*, I, Chapter 18
159 See references under 515.
161-62 *Summa Theologiae*, I, 13-5. Other references under 449-66
163 *Metaphysics*, II, Chapter 2. J. F. McCormick, S.J., *Natural Theology*, 52-53 and *passim*. G. Smith, S.J., *Natural Theology*, 96-100, 106-07, 120-22, 153. V. E. Smith, *Philosophical Physics*, 90-91, 120-25. *Summa Theologiae*, I, 2-3; I, 46-2 *ad* 7

14

Form and formal cause

Existence of form (164-67)

164 Everything which exists possesses form.
VARIANT Everything is formed and determinate.
NOTE In God and angels this does not mean it is an "informing" form. *confer* 168

165 Every individual nature can have only one substantial form.
NOTE Virtual plurality of forms is admissible. *confer* 20, 256, 537

166 Form is not in potency to form in the same order of being. *confer* 10

167 Material forms can exist only in matter.

Functions of form (168-72)

168 *The principle of hylemorphism*: Every natural body is one substance composed of two incomplete substantial principles, related to each other as potency and act, and called prime matter and substantial form. *confer* 255, 375

169 Matter and form are mutually proportionate.
VARIANTS A Form is realized in disposed matter (in its proper or proportionate potency). Hence, the principle of hylemorphism does not mean that it is bare prime matter which is informed by higher and living forms in substantial changes. *confer* 15, 379
B Every form is received, limited, and thus determined according to the nature of the matter or potency of which it is the form. *confer* 221, 363, 378

170 Matter acquires or loses being inasmuch as it acquires or loses form.

171 Form confers specific nature and all its consequences (powers, necessary properties, specific activity) on any reality.

172 Partial variants of 171. A Everything is *what* it is by its form.
B Form is the principle of specific difference. c Being follows form. *confer* 250 D Form informs the whole and all parts.
E The primary goodness of a thing is from its form; matter

participates in the goodness of the form. F Matter cannot exist without form; but some forms can exist without matter.

Form and the other causes (173-76)

173 The form is the intrinsic purpose of the thing.

VARIANTS A Form acts for its own good. B Forma est finis.

174 The intrinsic end is proportionate to form as the active principle tending to its own perfection.

VARIANT End corresponds to form. *confer* 132

APPLICATION A special application is: The end serves as form in moral matters and in choice. *confer* 233, 558

175 Form is the end of generation. *confer* 59-60

176 Every agent acts according to its form.

VARIANTS A Some inclination follows every form. B Every action proceeds in virtue of some form. c Activity follows form. *confer* 97, 171 D Form is the principle of specific action. *confer* 87c

NOTE In voluntary agents the agent's idea is the form which is the principle of purposeful action.

Forms in their hierarchy and continuity (177)

177 Forms (definitions, essences, species) are like cardinal numbers, each differing from the other by at least one essential characteristic, and virtually containing the perfections of the preceding lower number. *confer* 212-13

164-77 REFERENCES

For a general discussion of the functions of form: *On Being and Essence*, especially Chapters 2, 5-6. *Summa Theologiae*, I, 5-5; I, 50-5

164 *Summa Theologiae*, I, 7-2

165 M. Adler, *What Man Has Made of Man*, 190, note 35. *Contra Gentiles*, IV, Chapter 81 (reply to second objection)

166 *Summa Theologiae*, I, 77-1

169 *Summa Theologiae*, I, 76-5 *ad* 1, 3; I, 85-7; I-II, 63-1

171-72 *Summa Theologiae*, I, 7-2; I, 75-5 *ad* 3; I, 76-1, 8; I-II, 18-2. *Compendium of Theology*, I, Chapter 69. For further study of *Forma dat esse*, see *On Being and Essence*, Chapters 1, 4, 6, and (in Maurer edition and translation) footnote 12 of Chapter 1 and footnote 14 of Chapter 4.

176 *Summa Theologiae*, I, 3-2 (third reason); I, 15-1, 2; I, 76-2 *ad* 3; I, 85-2. *Contra Gentiles*, II, Chapter 20 (third argument)

15

Formal object

178 Acts, powers (or faculties), and habits are specified (immediately classified or specifically distinguished) by their formal objects to which they are essentially directed.

VARIANT The formal object specifies an operation as its end, term, or principle (agent). The type of activity in turn specifies the power that performs such an act. The power is characteristic of the nature. So, the formal object also in some way determines the nature of a being. *confer* 129-32, 207

COROLLARY Characteristic acts make the powers known to us.

179 Formal objects are specifically different only when they constitute a completely diverse object in its relation to a power. Contraries, as having a common aspect, pertain to the same formal object of a power. *confer* 82

180 The natural material object of any power is the whole range of objects in which the form of the formal object may be found. *confer* 308

178-80 REFERENCES

G. Klubertanz, S.J., *Philosophy of Human Nature,* 93, 99, 101, and numerous applications to the formal objects of senses, intellect, will, and habits throughout the book. *Summa Theologiae,* numerous citations and applications, especially I, 77-3; I-II, 8-2 *ad* 2, 3; I-II, 18-5; I-II, 54-2 *ad* 1; I-II, 62-2

Exercise 11
Formal objects

A State the formal object of each of these powers of man. The key is on pages 142-43.

1 agent intellect	6 motor power of the heart	10 power of nutrition
2 sight	7 common sense (unifying	11 irascible appetite
3 hearing	sense, central sense)	12 possible intellect
4 taste	8 concupiscible appetite	13 will
5 imagination	9 temperature sense	

B State the formal object of each of these habits.

1 art	9 botany	17 hope
2 philosophy	10 zoology	18 virtue of religion
3 metaphysics	11 medicine	19 habitual lying
4 ethics	12 profanity	20 synderesis
5 philosophy of nature	13 faith	21 political philosophy
6 prudence	14 justice	22 political science
7 anatomy	15 commutative justice	23 navigation
8 physiology	16 courage	24 tragedy

C Why is there no difference between the following, considered as powers or as habits?

1 will and free will
2 imagination and sense memory
3 knowledge of scholasticism and refutation of its opponents
4 study of health and of diseases

D Answer.

1 Why is the power of speech not a distinct power of man?
2 Why is the sense of pain not a distinct power of man?
3 Why does not the perception of melody prove a distinct power from the perception of tone?
4 Why is it doubtful whether kinesthetic sensations differ from pressure sensations sufficiently to constitute a distinct formal object?

16

Good and evil

Transcendental goodness (181-86)

181 Every being is good insofar as it is.

182 Every being seeks its own perfection, whether to preserve it, to improve it, to enjoy it, or to share it.

183 A Every being is in some way good to another being or other beings.

B Goodness spreads itself (for as a final cause it is the first of all causes from which all else proceeds).

184 *The principles of optimism* (summarizing 181-83): Every being, insofar as it is, is good to itself and to some other beings.

185 *Axiological principle*: The order of nature is essentially good. *confer* 430-34

186 The good of different natures is proportionately analogical to the diversity of natures.

Good and the causes (187-89)

187 The perfective good is an end.
VARIANT Only the good can motivate appetite. *confer* 127

188 Only the good can be a cause of being or of activity.

189 God's goodness is both the model, the source, and the end of all other goods. God is the common good of the universe.

Measures of perfection of the good (190-94)

190 Nature and the end are measures of the perfective and the (indifferent) useful good.

191 A The good of any creature consists in measure, form, and order.
B The good of any creature is a mean between excess and defect. *confer* 545

192 Unity is a measure of the perfection of a being. *confer* 538

193 Goodness results from integrity, evil results from any defect. See 232 for the sources of moral defect.
COROLLARY As the part is for the whole, any part is bad which is not conformed to the good of the whole.

194 The more general a good is, the more godlike it is. *confer* 183

Relationships and priorities among goods (195-98)

195 A person is the most excellent thing in nature. *confer* 438

196 The good of the whole is the good of the parts. *confer* 548

197 What befits a thing is the natural and immovable root of all else pertaining thereto.
VARIANT A partial variant is: The primary goodness of a thing is from its form.

198 Right order among goods requires that
A merely useful and pleasurable goods be subordinated to necessary (perfective) goods (that is, means, pleasures, and pains to ends)
B the part or organ be subordinated to its proper act
C less urgent needs and advantages be subordinated to more urgent needs

D the naturally imperfect or less perfect be subordinated to the better and more complete

E material goods be subordinated to spiritual goods

F things be subordinated to persons

G private advantage be subordinated to common good in the same order of goods

H social goods be subordinated to necessary personal goods

I civic goods be subordinated to necessary family goods

J the good of *mere* parts be subordinated to the good of the whole

K created goods be subordinated to the infinite good
confer 134, 138, 384

Evil—its relation to good (199-201)

199 Evil, though having neither being nor causal power of its own, is predicated of the good as its subject (of privation), and may be the occasion of good.

200 Evils arise from the deficient operation of finite causes.

201 God has a sufficient reason, the good, A for permitting the possibility of moral evil, and B for indirectly willing physical evil as a part of universal order.

181-201 REFERENCES

181-94 *Contra Gentiles*, III, Chapters 3, 16-17, 20, 24, 94. *Summa Theologiae*, I, 5-6; I, 19-2

183 J. Peghaire, C.S.Sp., "L'Axiome 'Bonum est diffusivum sui' dans le néo-platonisme et le thomisme," *Revue de l'Université d'Ottawa*, II (1930), 5-32

189 *Summa Theologiae*, I, 106-4; II-II, 26-3

190 *Summa Theologiae*, I-II, 18-4

195 *Contra Gentiles*, III, Chapters 11, 113

197 *Summa Theologiae*, I, 82-1; I, 5-6 *ad* 3; I-II, 18-2

198 *Politics*, I, Chapter 2 (a famous error). *Contra Gentiles*, III, Chapters 17 (fifth argument), 28, 94, 112-13. *Summa Theologiae*, I-II, 90-1; I-II, 96-4; II-II, 64-1; II-II, 66-1. See references under 138.

199-201 St. Augustine, *Confessions*, especially IV, Chapter 15; V, Chapter 10; VII, Chapters 2-3, 5, 12-13; VIII, Chapter 10. *Contra Gentiles*, III, Chapters 4-15, 71. *Summa Theologiae*, I, 14-10; I, 19-9; I, 48, 49

17

Habits

Nature of habits (202-04)

202 A disposition becomes or grows into a habit. Operative habits in particular are all acquired.

203 Only a being composite of potency and act is capable of acquiring habits.

204 The existence of operative habits may be recognized by three characteristics: A ease in the performance of a type of action; B consistency, accuracy, or stability in such performance; and C pleasure in such action.

COROLLARY Because of these characteristics, habits are said to be a second nature.

Source (205-06)

205 Like acts produce like habits in a disposed subject. *confer* 95, 362

206 Acquired operative habits are developed by repetition of similar acts, and if these be morally good habits, with repetition of the proper motive. *confer* 546

Distinctions (207-08)

207 Habits are generically distinguished by the powers which they perfect, and specifically distinguished by their formal objects. *confer* 83, 178, 541

208 No perfect moral habit excludes any other good moral habit. *confer* 543-44

NOTE For *morality* of habitual acts, see 245-46.

202-08 REFERENCES

General references: *Nicomachaean Ethics*, II, Chapters 1-6. J. Castiello, S.J., "The Psychology of Habit in St. Thomas," *Modern Schoolman*, XIV (1936), 8-12. G. Klubertanz, S.J., *Philosophy of Human Nature*, Chapter 12. *Summa Theologiae*, I-II, especially Questions 49-54

18
Hierarchy of being

Degrees or grades of being (209-11)

209 A thing is perfect to the degree that it is in act, and imperfect insofar as it is in potency. *confer* 23

210 In material and living bodies we find an ascending order of perfections in which the higher beings have their own perfections as well as those of the lower level of being. In the unity of the higher being the multiplicity of the lower beings is virtually present.

VARIANT A partial variant is: Life expresses itself as a unit and as a recapitulation of what has gone before it. *confer* 212-13

211 In the measure of its excellence of being, each being's nature, operations, and causal influence are more unified and reach out to more objects. *confer* 224

Principle of continuity—the chain of being (212-15)

212 The order of the universe displays a gradual scale of perfections from end to end through all essentially different intermediate steps.

213 Definitions (forms, essences, species) are like cardinal numbers, each differing from the other by at least one essential characteristic, and virtually containing the perfections of the preceding lower number. *confer* 177

214 Every superior nature in its least perfection or operation borders on the highest perfection or operation of the nature ranking next below it in the scale of being.

215 *Continuity of ends*: Divine Wisdom always joins the ends of the lower orders of being with the principles of the higher order. *confer* 154

Principle of plenitude (216-18)

216 By the free choice of the Creator the universe of being contains all essential levels of perfections and of natures.

217 The superior one is represented by many inferior beings.

218 An unattainable unity and fullness of the source is represented and imitated by variety and multiplicity in the lower orders of being. *confer* 220

Principle of participation (219-23)

219 That which exists by its essence is the cause of all that exists by participation in the same (analogous) type of perfection. *confer* 86

COROLLARY The unshared is therefore the original in a set of shared perfections.

NOTE While exemplary causality is primarily intended, in God's case efficient and final causality are also meant. Transcendental and pure perfections are especially meant.

220 Everything that is imperfect, multiple, composite, and varied in the lower rank of being is complete, one, simple, and unique in the highest or unparticipated rank of being.

VARIANT A partial variant is: The perfect precedes and is the measure of any class of perfections.

221 Being is participated according to the measure of the recipient essence.

COROLLARY All participated perfections are limited by and compounded with potency. *confer* 14, 378

222 Wherever there is diversity of rank or of excellence of perfections, the ranks show proportional analogy of the perfections. *confer* 38B, 219, 353

VARIANT A partial variant is: Things participate in and imitate the being and perfections of God at analogous and essentially diverse levels of perfection.

223 The more universal a good is, the more divine it is. *confer* 211

Primacy of the higher level of perfection (224-27)

224 In the *order of efficient causality*: A higher cause by simpler and fewer operations can do all that the lower cause performs by many and complex operations. *confer* 88-89, 211

225 In the *order of finality*:
A The universal and unparticipated end (supreme end) is the end of all other ends.
B The ends of the lower orders of being are subordinate to the ends of higher orders of being.
C The nearer a thing is to its end, the better it is.

226 The order of agents and the order of ends correspond. The subordination of agents corresponds to the subordination of ends. NOTE Application to end of persons over that of things (384); to primacy of will among the appetites (133, 144, 567).

227 Progress from lower to higher level of perfection must be a gift from above, not an unaided evolution from below. *confer* 87A

228 Criteria for judging degrees of perfection include: A comparative degree of act and potency (23, 209); B degree of immateriality (304); C comparative immanence of action; D range and depth of operation and causal influence and diffusion of goodness; E imperishability or freedom from substantial change; F unity and simplicity of structure in proportion to the scale of operations; G independent initiative and measure of liberty; H degree of natural control of other things.
NOTE For hierarchy of societies, see principles of pluralism and subsidiarity, 508-09.

209-28 REFERENCES

General references: L.-B. Geiger, O.P., *La Participation dans la Philosophie de S. Thomas d'Aquin*, especially Appendix I of 1953 edition, the entries on the principles. E. Gilson, *Philosophy of St. Thomas Aquinas* (translation of third French edition), 83, 88-89, 92, 130-31, 136-37, 156-57, 160-63, 169, 266, 272-76. Sister Mary Dominica Mullen, *Essence and Operation in the Teaching of St. Thomas and in Some Modern Philosophies*, Chapter 5. V. E. Smith, *Idea-Men of Today*, Chapter 16

209 *On Being and Essence*, Chapter 4, near end; Chapter 5. *Contra Gentiles*, I, Chapter 43, "Item. Tanto . . ."; III, Chapter 20. *Compendium of Theology*, I, Chapter 80

210 M. Adler, *What Man Has Made of Man*, 176, note 23. *Summa Theologiae*, I, 47-2; I, 76-3 (virtual presence). *On the Nature of Matter*, Chapter 4

211 *Summa Theologiae*, I, 56-1; I, 57-2; I, 77-2. *Contra Gentiles*, II, Chapter 6 (sixth argument). *Compendium of Theology*, I, Chapter 22

212 *Summa Theologiae*, I, 18-3; I, 50-1; I, 78-1. *Contra Gentiles*, II, Chapter 95

213 *What Man Has Made of Man*, 183, note 31. *Metaphysics*, VIII, Chapter 3. *Summa Theologiae*, I, 47-2; I, 50-3, 4; I, 76-5

214-15 *Contra Gentiles*, II, Chapter 68 (sixth paragraph to end); III, Chapter 22 (for man)

216 *Summa Theologiae*, I, 19-3, 4; I, 25-6; I, 47-1. *On the Power of God*, 1-5. For an amazing misunderstanding of the principle of plenitude, see A. Lovejoy, *The Great Chain of Being*, and comment in A. C. Pegis, *Saint Thomas and the Greeks*.

217-18, *Summa Theologiae*, I, 47-1. *Contra Gentiles*, II, Chapters 45-46; III, Chapters 20,
220 97; IV, Chapter 1 (third paragraph). *Compendium of Theology*, I, Chapters 72, 102

219 *Metaphysics*, II, Chapter 1. *Contra Gentiles*, I, Chapter 40 (second argument). *Summa Theologiae*, I, 2-3 (fourth way); I, 6-4 (last paragraph); I, 44-1; I, 65-1; I, 103-1 (in which final cause is considered). *On the Power of God*, 3-5

222 *Summa Theologiae*, I, 13-5; I, 93-1, 2

223 *Contra Gentiles*, III, Chapters 24, 69

224 *Truth*, 8-3 *ad* 12 (applied to attainment of goodness)

225 *Summa Theologiae*, I, 96-1. *Contra Gentiles*, III, Chapters 25, 37. *Compendium of Theology*, I, Chapter 148

226 *Summa Theologiae*, I-II, 109-6. *Contra Gentiles*, III, Chapter 17, "Item. Ad ordinem . . ." *On the Power of God*, 7-2 *ad* 10

228 On immanence: *Summa Theologiae*, I, 18-3, 4. *Contra Gentiles*, IV, Chapter 11. On immateriality: *Summa Theologiae*, I, 14-1. *Compendium of Theology*, I, Chapter 75. On incorruptibility: *Truth*, 5-3, 8. On unity and simplicity: *Contra Gentiles*, IV, Chapter 1 (third paragraph). *Truth*, 8-3 *ad* 12

19

Human acts

229 A human act requires intellectual knowledge of the object or purpose of the act, deliberation, and choice. According to the degree of their freedom in acting, men are responsible both for their human acts and for the normally foreseeable consequences of these. Whatever diminishes freedom proportionally diminishes responsibility. *confer* 566, 241-46

230 A The ultimate constitutive norm of morality is the Divine Nature.

B The proximate constitutive norm of the morality of human acts is human nature considered completely, both in itself and in all its essential relationships. *confer* 383

231 The determinants of a good or evil act in the concrete are these three: A the object of the act, B the intention of the agent, and C intrinsic circumstances modifying or qualifying either the object or the intention.

NOTE No thing as a thing is morally good or morally evil. In other words, moral ends are accidental to natural things which receive their moral quality only from being willed.

232 An act is good if its whole cause is good; it is evil from any defect. The act in other words must not violate any factor of the norm of morality either in the object of the act, the intention of the agent, or intrinsic circumstances. *confer* 193

VARIANT Bonum ex integra causa; malum ex quolibet defectu.

COROLLARY Every part is bad which is not conformed to the whole.

233 The object is the primary determinant of the moral quality and of the species of the act considered by itself; the intention is the primary determinant of the species and of the merit or malice of the entire act. *confer* 76

NOTE The end serves as the form in moral matters. *confer* 558

234 Some of the chief classes of intrinsically evil human acts are:

A acts which would necessarily frustrate the supreme purpose of human life (for example, contempt of God)

B acts which would necessarily cause disorder or destruction to innocent life (for example, murder, suicide)

C acts which necessarily violate others' natural rights (for example, robbing the poor)

D acts which necessarily frustrate the achievement of the natural end of a natural power (for example, lying, contraception) *confer* 393

E acts which necessarily tend to destroy or endanger the substance of the common good (for example, treason)

235 Every human act in the concrete has a moral quality because of the intention of the agent.

236 Knowledge of evil is not in itself evil.

237 Every direct choice of evil is morally evil.

VARIANTS A Evil is not to be done that good may come of it.
B A good intention does not justify the use of evil means for the end in view.

238 Good is not to be done that evil may come from it.

239 A seriously evil human act requires a gravely evil object (or one estimated to be such), sufficient reflection for recognition of the serious evil and to allow choice of the opposite, and the following choice of the known evil. (The evil commanded act need not follow.)

240 A We are not obliged to avoid the remote occasions of sin, particularly not all of them.

B We are obliged to avoid all voluntary (unnecessary) proximate occasions of sin.

c In necessary (not chosen) proximate occasions of sin we are obliged to make the occasion (the danger of sinning) remote.

Some rules on modifications of human acts (241-46)

241 Involuntary ignorance of the evil nature of an act, as well as its equivalent states of forgetfulness, narcosis, hypnosis, insanity, and so on, weakens the voluntariness of an act performed in such ignorance, and excuses a person from guilt in as far as the sinfulness of the deed is inculpably unknown. This applies to ignorance both of law and of fact.

242 Every one has the duty to know the main principles of the natural law and the duties of his state in life or office. Ignorance of these duties is vincible; if prolonged, is culpable. Acts performed or neglected during or because of such ignorance are culpable.

243 Passion (emotion) preceding a human act, though increasing voluntariness, tends to decrease deliberation and freedom, and so diminishes responsibility in the measure of the intensity of the passion. But it rarely removes all reasoned choice. Fear also diminishes, but probably never destroys choice.

244 Acts performed under duress or unjust external violence inducing grave fear probably never destroy voluntariness or choice. But the injustice of such violence is usually cause for positive law voiding obligations and consequences of such acts.

245 Acts performed from habit are voluntary in cause, at least as long as the habit is desired or allowed to continue.

246 An act performed out of an evil habit may have diminished freedom and responsibility if the person is meeting his obligation of trying to break the habit.

247 *Merit*

A An act meriting a reward from God must be free, good (virtuous), performed in this life, pleasing to God, and accepted by God.

B An act meriting a reward from a fellow man must be a deed or omission that is not already due to him in justice.

248 *Principle of twofold effect*: One may permit and perform an act that has both a good and an evil effect foreseen as flowing from it when all these conditions are together verified:

A The agent directly intends only the good, and merely permits the evil.

B The act itself is morally good or morally indifferent.

C The good effect of the act precedes or is simultaneous with the evil effect. (The good effect is causally independent of the evil.)

D The good effect surpasses or is morally equal to the permitted evil effect.

Note that the conditions may be expressed negatively:

A The agent may not intend the evil.

B The act itself may not be evil (intrinsically).

C The evil effect may not be the cause of the good effect.

D The evil effect may not surpass the good effect.

249 As a contract consists of two or more human and moral acts performed by each of two or more persons, the meeting of minds and wills needed for a valid contract requires that:

A the parties when contracting be capable of a human act and be juridically eligible to contract in this matter with this person or persons

B the parties have sufficient knowledge of the same object of agreement

C the parties give true (free, not unjustly coerced) and internal consent of the will

D the consent be mutually signified, morally simultaneous, and externally expressed

E the object of consent be physically and morally possible, ethically right (not immoral, not unjust), and juridically possible (that is, be one's own goods, alienable or transferable goods, valuable, and legally permitted)

APPLICATION The application of the principles of contract to marriage gives us the well-known maxims: A Consent makes the marriage. B Marriage is valid only between juridically eligible parties.

NOTE See 67, notes F, G, and I, on doubts in contracts.

229-49 REFERENCES

General discussions: T. J. Higgins, S.J., *Man as Man,* Chapters 3-4. E. Gilson, *Philosophy of St. Thomas Aquinas* (translation of third French edition), Chapters 14-15. *Summa Theologiae,* I-II, especially Questions 6-7, 17-21, 24, 34, 71, 73, 76-78

230 Morals according to nature: *Contra Gentiles,* III, Chapter 129. The Thomistic formula of "right reason": *Summa Theologiae,* I-II, 18-5; I-II, 19-3, 4, 5; I-II, 21-1, 2; I-II, 64-3; I-II, 65-1; II-II, 8-3 *ad* 3; II-II, 17-1

233 *Summa Theologiae,* I-II, 1-3; I-II, 18-6; I-II, 75-4; II-II, 23-8

237 Variants: Plato, *Crito.* L. Walker, S.J., Machiavelli's *Discourses,* I, 118-28, discussing Machiavelli's use of the maxim

240 G. Kelly, S.J., *Modern Youth and Chastity*

241-46 *Nicomachaean Ethics,* III, Chapters 1-5

247 *Summa Theologiae,* I-II, 21-3, 4; I-II, 62-4, 9

248 J. C. Ford, S.J., *Theological Studies,* VI (1945), 532-37. *Man as Man,* 154-58, 399-400, 503, 665-78, 969

249 *Man as Man,* Chapters 19 and 22, Section V

20

The human soul

250 The human soul, as a subsistent substantial form in man, communicates to the body its own act of existence and is the principle by which man has every essential grade of his perfection: as a man, as an animal, as a living thing, as a body, as a substance, and as a being. *confer* 171, 258, and Thomistic thesis 16

251 The soul is the total principle of only the spiritual powers and the spiritual operations of the man; the composite of body and soul is the principle of operations of the vegetative and sensitive orders. *confer* Thomistic thesis 17

252 The whole corporeal nature is subject to the soul and is related to it as its matter and instrument.

253 The soul is the noblest of forms.

254 The intellectual soul in a certain way is all things.
VARIANT   The intellectual soul is the form of all forms. *confer* 320

250-54 REFERENCES

250 *Summa Theologiae,* I, 75-2, 5 *ad* 3; I, 76-1 *ad* 5; I, 76-4. *Contra Gentiles,* II, Chapters 58-60

251 *Summa Theologiae,* I, 77-5, 6

254 *On the Soul,* III, Chapter 8. *Summa Theologiae,* I, 14-1; I, 80-1; I, 81-2 *ad* 2

21
Hylemorphism

255 *The principle of hylemorphism* or the principle of matter-form: Every natural body is one substance composed of two incomplete substantial principles, related to each other as potency and act, and called prime matter and substantial form. *confer* 168, 375

256 There is only one substantial form in each natural body. But other perfections or forms of the compound may in some instances be virtually present. *confer* 20, 165, 512, 537

257 The principles of a natural body are matter, form, and privation. *confer* 57-60

258 *The principle or doctrine of vitalism*: In living bodies the form is the intrinsic ultimate substantial principle of life; this vital principle or soul is really distinct from and really united with the matter of the body as its first actuality; and it specifies the type of life.

259 A living body is essentially distinct from and essentially superior to a nonliving natural body.

260 Since the relation of matter to form is a relation of potency to act, every relation of potency to act in both the real and logical orders may be termed analogously a relation of matter to form. *confer* 381

255-60 REFERENCES

255-57 *Physics*, I, Chapters 7-9; II, Chapters 1, 7. *On Generation and Corruption*, II, Chapter 9. *Metaphysics*, V, Chapter 2; VII, Chapters 3, 7-8, 17; VIII, Chapters 1-4; XII, Chapters 2-4. Brother Benignus Gerrity, F.S.C., *Nature, Knowledge, and God*, Chapters 2 and especially 6-7. J. F. McCormick, S.J., *Scholastic Metaphysics*, Chapters 10 and especially 11. V. E. Smith, *Philosophical Physics*, 58-75, 205-08, 217-31

258 *On the Soul*, II, Chapters 1-2, 4. *Nature, Knowledge, and God*, Chapter 8. G. Klubertanz, S.J., *Philosophy of Human Nature*, Chapters 2-3. *Scholastic Metaphysics*, Chapter 12. *Summa Theologiae*, I, 18-1, 2; I, 75-1

22

Hypothesis

261 An hypothesis must be probable (not in conflict with other truths and not leading to consequences against the facts), useful (as guiding and suggesting further research and experiment), and capable of being further tested. *confer* 157, 521, 534

23

Inferences

Conversion of propositions (262-63)

262 Propositions legitimately converted are either both true or both false.

263 Conversion is legitimate when (1) E and I propositions are simply converted; and (2) A and E propositions are accidentally (partially) converted.

Immediate inferences of opposed propositions (264-73)

264 Contradictory propositions cannot be both true nor both false, but one of them must be true and the other false. *confer* 34
VARIANT There is only one proper contradictory of each proposition.

265 Hence, from the truth of one the falsity of the contradictory follows; and from the falsity of one the truth of the contradictory follows.

266 One contradictory fact proves the falsity of a strictly universal contradictory proposition. *confer* 156

267 Contrary propositions cannot both be true, but may both be false. *confer* 33

268 From the truth of one contrary the falsity of its contrary follows; but from the falsity of one contrary nothing follows in regard to the truth or falsity of the other contrary.

269 Subcontrary propositions cannot both be false.

270 Hence, from the falsity of one follows the truth of the other sub-contrary.

271 As subaltern propositions are not in mutual opposition, they can be both true and both false.

272 From the truth of the universal proposition follows the truth of the corresponding particular; but from the truth of the particular the truth of the universal does not follow. *confer 287*

273 From the falsity of the universal the falsity of its subaltern does not follow; but from the falsity of the particular the falsity of the corresponding universal proposition follows.

Immediate modal inferences (274-81)

A *Metaphysical bases of modal inferences*

274 That which is can be.

275 That which can be may or may not be actual.

276 What cannot be is not.

277 What must be is and can be.

278 What can be or not-be does not need to be.

279 What may be also may not-be.

280 What is not will never have to be.

281 All that can be need not simultaneously be nor be simultaneously possible nor be simultaneously actual.

B *Logical formulae of 274-81*

274 The inference from the fact of existence to possibility of being is valid. Hence, if the first is true, the second is true. But inference from existence to *mere* possibility of existence is not valid.

275 The inference from possibility of existence to actual existence is not valid. Also, the inference from contingent being to existence is not valid.

276 The inference from impossibility of being to nonexistence is valid.

277 The inference from necessary existence to existence, actuality, and possibility (not *mere* possibility) of existence is valid.

280 The inference from nonexistence at any time and from change of existence to a lack of necessary existence is valid.

281 From simultaneous multiple possibility there does not follow the possibility of the simultaneous existence of their corresponding actualities.

Inferences from predicates or attributes (282-85)

282 *Dictum de nota notae*: A known attribute of an attribute or part is also an attribute of the thing itself. (Nota notae est nota rei ipsius.)

VARIANT Whatever is true of the accident or power is also true of the form or substance in which it inheres. *confer* 454-55

283 A valid inference is drawn from a less universal predicate to a more universal predicate of the same perfection in affirmative propositions, but not in negative propositions.

284 A valid inference is drawn from a more universal predicate to a less universal predicate in the same line of perfection in negative propositions, but not in affirmative propositions.

285 A valid inference is drawn from a privative predicate to a negative predicate of the same line of perfection in all types of propositions.

286 The converse of a mutual relationship is as true or false as the prior proposition stating that relationship.

Mediate inferences: proof (287-301)

287 *Dictum de omni et nullo* (sometimes referred to as the principle of subsumption): Whatever is affirmed or denied universally of any subject is thereby affirmed or denied of every logical part of that subject.

Original formula: Quod dicitur de omni dicitur de singulis; quod dicitur de nullo negatur de singulis (membris). Literally: What is said of all (in a given class) is said of each of them; what is said of none (in the class) is denied of each of them.

288 *Evidence* for judgments and proof:

A Every judgment must be based on evidence. *confer* 313

B But self-evident judgments do not need demonstration. *confer* 298B

289 No argument or conclusion contrary to the evident facts is valid.

290 An hypothesis or explanation which contradicts evident facts is not rationally tenable. *confer* 261

291 Without a sufficient reason (that is, sufficient evidence) nothing should be affirmed or denied, or held as true or false or certain. *confer* 35B

292 *The principle of economy*:
A An explanation that accounts for all the facts in terms of a single or a few principles is preferable to the more complex theory. An explanation of any phenomenon is to be regarded as better and truer in which the minimum number of factors, the fewer steps in a process, and more immediate causes are included. *confer* 433

B In identifying an unseen cause of a phenomenon, the least cause capable of explaining the phenomenon must be accepted. In other words, a proportionate cause is required and suffices. For example: Miracles must not be postulated as an explanation of an event when a natural cause suffices in the circumstances.
VARIANT A demonstration of the necessary truth of some unseen cause, reason, or theory requires proof both of the necessity and suitability of the explanation offered and the exclusion of the other attempted explanations.

C In psychology, the principle of economy is known as Morgan's Canon. "In no case may we interpret an action as the outcome of the exercise of a higher psychical faculty, if it can be interpreted as the outcome of the exercise of one which stands lower in the psychological scale."

D In physical sciences, the principle of economy is referred to as the minimal principle or as Maupertois' axiom of least action. Nature tends to operate along lines of minimum distance, shortest time, and with the least expenditure of force required for the given situation.

E Distinctions between species, individuals, and constituents of beings are not to be multiplied without good reason. *confer* 79

293 *The principle of identity and difference*: We ought to affirm as true the mutual identity of natures (or concepts or terms) which are the same as a third with which they are compared; we ought to deny their identity if one is the same as the third and the other is different from this same third nature (or concept or term). *confer* 78, 370

294 Accidents manifest the substance to which they belong. *confer* 327, 516-17

295 Every effect when known can lead to some knowledge of the existence, power, and nature of its cause or causes. *confer* 108
VARIANT The effect may be used instead of a definition in proving the existence of a cause.

296 Only from the present influence of a cause or the present dependence of the effect on it is the present existence of the cause to be directly inferred. *confer* 109

297 Demonstration follows the weaker premise.
NOTE This rule applies to extension, quality, certitude or probability, clarity, and so on, of the conclusion.

298 Infinite series in argument:
A All proof must be ultimately reducible to self-evident premises.
B The demand for an infinite series of premises and the rejection of any self-evident premises is unreasonable and skeptical.

299 The proof of a conditional proposition requires proof of the connection or dependence of the conditioned upon the condition.

300 A proof based on experience is a proof of facts, and so must be supported by concrete instances in experience.

301 *Arguments based on analogy*:
A What is similar to one member of a set of like things is probably also true (or false) in the other members.
B To like causes correspond like effects.
C Like and unlike things have like and unlike properties, effects, and causes.
D An inference based on analogy has greater probability according to the greater degree of likeness between the compared objects.
E Quantitative likenesses are least significant, qualitative and structural likenesses are more significant.
NOTE See also *Syllogisms* and truth in argument, 534.

261-301 REFERENCES
261 G. H. Joyce, S.J., *Principles of Logic,* Chapter 13 and pages 350, 399-400
262-86 *Principles of Logic,* 84-104, or in any larger logic book
263 *Prior Analytics,* I, Chapters 2-3
264 *On Interpretation,* Chapters 7, 10. *Rhetoric,* II, Chapter 19. *Summa Theologiae,* I-II, 67-3
274-81 *On Interpretation,* Chapters 12-13
281 *Metaphysics,* IX, Chapters 5, 9
282 *Prior Analytics,* I, Chapter 27. *Categories,* Chapter 3

287 *Principles of Logic,* 187-91
288 *Posterior Analytics,* I, Chapters 10, 13; II, Chapters 4, 9. *Topics,* I, Chapter 1. *Metaphysics,* IV, Chapters 3-6. V. E. Smith, *Philosophical Physics,* 41-42
292 *Posterior Analytics,* I, Chapter 25. *On the Soul,* III, Chapter 9. F. Harmon, *Principles of Psychology* (1951 edition), 402, referring to C. L. Morgan. *Principles of Logic,* 349-53, citing Newton's Rules I and II. *Summa Theologiae,* I, 78-4
294 See 516-17.
295 *Summa Theologiae,* I, 2-2c and *ad* 2
296 *Posterior Analytics,* I, Chapter 13; II, Chapters 12, 16
298B *Posterior Analytics,* I, Chapters 19-22, 24
301 *Principles of Logic,* 259-63

Exercise 12
The principle of economy

Directions: Supplement 292 with 291, 79, 84, 427, and 433. The problems in this exercise are very interesting but often require specific information from philosophy or from the history of science. The key is on pages 144-46.

1 Plants do not sense. How do we know this?
2 Animals have no intelligence. How do we know this?
3 Man has no innate ideas. Why do we deny innate ideas to man?
4 The soul in man is only one. Why have we not a second or third soul as Plato and others have thought?
5 The soul has not evolved from matter or some pre-existing condition, but is created in each instance. Why?
6 The human soul had no pre-existence in some former life or world. Why not?
7 Telepathy is not a miraculous phenomenon.
8 Stigmatic phenomena are sometimes due to hysteria or pathological conditions, and not to God's miraculous action.
9 A greater simplicity in explaining the movements of planets largely accounted for the acceptance of the Copernican sun-centered system and the abandonment of the Ptolemaic earth-centered system. Why does this fit scientific thinking?
10 One sincerely seeking the truth should accept neither gratis assertions nor gratis denials.
11 Some of the cures at Lourdes are wonderful but not accepted as surely miraculous by the board of doctors who certify miracles. What factors of evidence or proof may be missing?

12 Why do scientists accept the view of one law of gravity operating in the same way throughout the universe?

13 Why has the Aristotelian hypothesis of successive souls in man—vegetative, then animal, then human—been discarded by modern thinkers with fuller embryological evidence?

14 Though we need an agent intellect to explain intellectual knowledge, we do not need an agent sense to explain sensory knowledge.

15 Why do we say that space is not a reality distinct from bodies that are said to be in space?

16 Study the proof of creation of the world. Why does it proceed by way of elimination of hypotheses of noncreation, evolution, pantheistic emanation?

17 Why did St. Thomas believe that one could from reason prove neither the eternal nor the temporal origin of the world, even though one can prove its creation?

18 Show that there are only mental distinctions between:

A power and holiness in God

B God as Supreme Being and God as Creator of all beings

C the human soul and its immortality

D animality and rationality in man (or more generally, between the parts of an essential definition)

E action and passion (see axioms 27-30)

19 Is the principle of economy being used when one claims that men have only those natural rights which human destiny and nature require?

20 St. Thomas thought that life arose from nonlife by action of the heavenly bodies. Pasteur's experiments with bacterial and microscopic life refuted this theory and set up the more modern view that all life comes from life. What was St. Thomas' mistake? Why is Pasteur right in his thinking?

21 From the principle of economy and from rules on specification of powers by formal objects show that there are not two powers in man:

A not both a will and a free will

B not both an imagination and a sensory memory of past sensations

confer Exercise 11, C, 1-2

22 Show that no human being is essentially superior to any other human being.

24
Knowledge

302 Knowledge, the highest form of life, is the living intentional possession of the forms of other things as other.

303 Nothing is in the human intellect which was not first in the sense. VARIANT The principle of our knowledge is from sense. Note the following connections: A No innate knowledge; the human mind at the start of life is "a blank sheet." B Proof begins from sensible existents. C Function of the agent intellect. D Extrinsic dependence of the soul on the body. E Analogical character of our knowledge of the spiritual and of God. F Connatural object of the human intellect in 309.

304 The immateriality of things is the measure of their degree of cognoscibility (intelligibility); the immateriality of the knower is the measure of his capacity for knowing.

305 The actually known is immediately united to a knower. *confer* 317, 319

306 Any particular fixed modification of a sense would impede knowledge of any things other than the same kind of particular determination.

Objects of knowledge (307-11)

307 Being is the formal object of the intellect.

308 All things that are or that can be conceived as being are the material objects of the intellect. *confer* 254

309 The essences of material things are the connatural object of the human intellect.

310 Singulars and the accidents of material things are the only field of the senses.

311 The known form specifies each act of knowledge.

Dependence on the object or the correspondence theory (312-14)

312 Truth (logical) requires that the mind conform to things as the measure of the truth of knowledge. *confer* 368

313 *Principle of evidence*: The objective evidence of being is the criterion of the truth of assent and the motive for certitude in assent. *confer* 155

314 Species, both sensible and intelligible, are the medium by which we know, not the medium in which we know. The species (concepts) are pure signs, not instrumental signs.

Union of known with knower (315-20)

315 True knowledge is the child of object and knower.

316 Knowledge is an assimilation of the knower to the known.
VARIANT Knowledge is an intentional union of knower with known. *confer* 302

317 The objects of cognitive powers become present in the knower by their likenesses (species, intentions, or forms) impressed on the cognitive power.
VARIANTS A The species is the principle of knowing. B The likeness of the known is in the knower. C The knower is united to the known by means of a species or likeness which is a pure sign or medium by which we know. *confer* 302, 314
Note the special sense in which this must be applied to God's knowledge and the angels' self-knowledge. The maxim is unqualified for human and animal knowledge.

318 The known is in the knower according to the nature of the knower. (Cognitum est in cognoscente secundum modum cognoscentis.) *confer* 378

319 The known in act (as known) is the knower in act (as knowing). Hence: A The sensible (object) in act is the sense in act (as sensing). B The intelligible (object) in act is the intellect in act (as understanding).

320 The soul (or intellect) by understanding becomes in a certain way all things.
VARIANT The soul is the place of forms or the form of forms. *confer* 254, 302

Universals (321-22)

321 The universal (that is, the object of a universal concept) is formally in the mind, fundamentally (or materially) in similar finite things. *confer* 160

322 Abstraction of the essence of an immediately experienced thing is not falsification.

Relations of knowledge to appetite (323-26)

confer 553-57

323 Knowledge precedes appetitive activity in time and causality.

324 An appetite is a necessary concomitant and complement of a cognitive power.

325 Knowledge is of things in the measure in which their forms exist representatively in the intellect. Appetite tends to things as they exist in themselves. *confer* 556

VARIANTS A Knowing is intentional possession; willing is tendential possession. B Truth, the object of the intellect, is representatively in the intellect; good, the object of the will, is in things.

326 Intellectual knowledge is better than acts of will in regard to goods that are inferior to or equal to the knower's nature; it may be less excellent than acts of will in regard to higher goods only analogically known by the intellect.

Mode of cognoscibility (327-30)

327 Substances (essences, natures) are known by human intellects in and from their operations and accidents. *confer* 294, 516-17

328 Potency is known only through act. *confer* 4

329 Active powers are revealed by their acts or by their specific formal objects.

330 Causes are revealed by their effects. *confer* 108

302-30 REFERENCES

On the Soul, especially II, Chapters 5, 12; III, Chapters 2-8. *Metaphysics,* X, Chapters 1, 6 (on the notion of measure). G. Klubertanz, S.J., *Philosophy of Human Nature,* especially Chapters 4, 8. J. Pieper, *The Human Wisdom of St. Thomas,* 24-35. Principles recurring often in *Summa Theologiae:* I, 12; I, 13-1, 8; I, 14; I, 16; I, 77; I, 79; I, 84-87; I, 89. *Truth,* 1-3, 10. F. D. Wilhelmsen, *Man's Knowledge of Reality,* especially Part II, "Judgment and Truth"

Exercise 13
Knowledge

A Complete the seven statements on the next page. The key is on page 146.

1 The universal is . . . in things, . . . in the intellect.

2 The soul . . . is all things.

3 The known is in the knower according . . .

4 The actually known is . . .

5 Truth is in . . . ; good is in . . .

6 The species in the knower represents . . . of the known.

7 Human intellects know substance . . .

B Citations.

8 Cite the principle on the origin of human knowledge.

9 Cite the principle on immateriality in knowledge.

10 Cite the principle of evidence.

11 Name the objects of sensory knowledge.

12 Name the formal, material, and connatural objects of the human intellect.

C Revise these incorrect citations.

13 Species is that which we know.

14 Appetite precedes knowledge.

15 Intellectual knowledge is always better than volition.

16 The cognitive powers complement the appetitive powers of the same order (that is, of the sensory or the intellectual order).

17 The known in potency is the knower in potency.

18 Knowledge possesses other things insofar as they are identical with the knower.

25
Law

Law in general (331-34)

331 Law is and must be an act of the practical reason.

332 Law is only a means to the common good of the community.

333 No law can bind a subject to do the impossible or anything morally evil. *confer* 337c, 484

334 Affirmative precepts of the law bind ever but only in every due act; negative precepts bind ever and for every act.
VARIANTS A Affirmative precepts of the law bind continuously but not continually; negative precepts bind continuously and

continually. B Affirmative precepts of the law bind always and on every due occasion, but not in every act; negative precepts bind always, on all occasions, and in every act.

Natural law (335-36)

335 The natural law is prior to any positive law, and is the basis and criterion of the justice of all positive laws. *confer* 337B, 491

336 The primary and unifying principle of the law is: Do the necessary good; avoid evil.

VARIANTS A The rational subject must will only that good which is according to right reason. B Right order is good and must be kept and not disturbed. *confer* 383

NOTE This primary judgment or principle of the practical order is comparable to the principle of contradiction (33) in the speculative order.

Positive law (337-42)

337 Positive law is true law only when it A is an act of legitimate authority; B is just; c is physically and morally possible of observance; and D is properly promulgated.

In other words, these principles together must be observed:

A The lawgiver and law enforcer must have jurisdiction over the subjects and over the matter or content of the law.

B No higher law may be contravened.

c 1 Necessity knows no law. *confer* 333

  2 A positive law is not binding in particular instances when its observance entails difficulties disproportionate to the importance and purpose of the law.

D Doubtful laws do not bind. *confer* 67

NOTE The debated conditions of community consent and of enforceability are omitted here, especially as most recent scholastics do not require these elements.

338 Unless an unjust positive law commands evil or forbids a necessary good, it may be obeyed for reasons of prudence and the common good.

339 In interpreting law, burdens must be considered in a restrictive sense and favors must be considered in a generous sense.

340 Positive law is not concerned with trifles.

341 Laws justly declaring an incapacity to act or to receive benefits invalidate the attempted act or reception even if they are inculpably unknown or facts pertaining to their application in a concrete instance are unknown.

342 In a conflict of laws, the higher law prevails. *confer* 384, 495

331-42 REFERENCES

Substantial discussions of law are found in almost any scholastic text on ethics. T. J. Higgins, S.J., *Man as Man,* especially Chapter 27. Pope Leo XIII, *Human Liberty (Libertas Praestantissimum). Summa Theologiae,* I-II, especially Questions 90, 91, 93-2, 94-2, 95, 96, 97

334 J. Messner, *Social Ethics,* 209-12, on the four relations of natural to positive law. *Summa Theologiae,* II-II, 3-2; I-II, 71-5 *ad* 3; I-II, 100-10 *ad* 2

336 For other suggestions on formulating this primary principle, see *Man as Man,* No. 236.

337 *Summa Theologiae,* I-II, 96-4, 6 (last sentence)

338 *Truth,* 17-5

26

Learning and recall

The laws of association or the primary laws of learning (343-45)

343 *Law of similarity:* A subject tends to associate mental data or conscious states of feeling and action which are alike in some way.

344 *Law of contrast:* A subject tends to associate mental data and conscious activities which are opposite in nature or in meaning.

345 *Law of contiguity* (proximity): A subject tends to associate certain events, internal or external, which occurred together (near each other) in time or place.

Secondary laws (346-49)

Modern formulations chiefly from Thorndike.

346 *Law of exercise:* Practice of a response favors its acquisition or retention, while lack of exercise leads to forgetting. *confer* 206

347 *Law of effect:* Responses tend to be repeated or avoided in proportion to the satisfaction or dissatisfaction that they afford a subject.

348 *Law of primacy:* Other things being equal, the first steps in a series of responses are learned better and retained better.

349 *Law of recency*: Other things being equal, responses that have been more recently exercised tend to be repeated more readily than those which have been exercised less recently.

343-49 REFERENCES

Memory and Reminiscence, Chapter 2. F. Harmon, *Principles of Psychology* (1951 edition), Chapter 14

27

Likeness (exemplarism, imitation)

Exemplary causality (350-57)

350 *Principle of exemplarism*: In the adequate causality of any contingent being, a model or exemplary form must be included.
VARIANT Every agent acts according to a model form.

351 The thing modeled (the copy) must be like the exemplar according to the form (idea) of the exemplar, but not necessarily according to its mode of being. *confer 96*

352 The unity and infinity of God's being is represented and imitated by multiple lower orders of being. *confer 218*

353 All creatures analogically resemble God. *confer 222*

354 The exemplar is the principle of likeness; the image is the term of likeness.

355 Because of his spiritual soul, his intellect and will, and their acts of knowing and loving God, man is said to be an image of God. *confer 438*

356 Everything is perfect according to the degree of its likeness to its principle.
NOTE This also applies to effect and efficient cause. *confer 225, 228*

357 *Principle of mimesis*: Art imitates nature.
NOTE Application to political arts in 507.

Likeness in relation to agent and end (358-65)

358 Every cause in acting produces a thing somewhat like itself. *confer 60, 95*

359 Like natures perform like functions and have like natural intrinsic ends. *confer* 112, 146

360 The living body generates only its own like or members of its own species. *confer* 95

361 Like powers have like formal objects and perform like acts.

362 Like acts produce habits like themselves. *confer* 205

363 The likeness of the agent is received into the patient according to the nature of the patient. *confer* 169, 221, 378

364 An agent does not act on its own like or equal. *confer* 90, 104

365 All things desire (tend) to be like God.

Knowledge and truth (366-69)

366 Knowledge of effects leads to the knowledge of their causes as far as they are like their effects. *confer* 108, 330

367 The likeness of the known is in the knower according to the mode of being of the knower. *confer* 317-18

368 Knowledge resembles reality or "intentionally" corresponds to reality. *confer* 312

369 The reason for the intelligibility of a being is its likeness to the idea of its maker. *confer* 36, 526

Predication of likeness (370-71)

370 *Principle of identity and difference,* ontological formula: Things like to one and the same thing are like to each other.
Principle of identity and difference, logical formula: We ought to affirm as true the mutual identity of two natures (or concepts or terms) which are the same as a third with which they are compared; we ought to deny their identity if one is the same as the third and the other is different from this same third nature (or concept or term). *confer* 293

371 Things mutually alike may be said to be like each other. But things in different orders are not properly said to be like each other; the inferior or dependent is rightly said to be like the superior or source, not vice versa. *confer* 413, 459

Virtue and rights (372-74)

372 Likeness belongs to virtue, for there is no virtue without love of virtue. *confer* 546

373 Like rejoices in its own kind.

374 The natural likeness and equality of man extends to origin, nature, destiny, and rights based on nature and destiny. *confer* 444, 492

350-74 REFERENCES

350 H. Renard, S.J., *Philosophy of Being* (second edition), 161-64. *Summa Theologiae,* I, 14-8; I, 15; I, 22-1; I, 44-3; I-II, 93-1. *Truth,* 3-1, 2, 3
351 *Summa Theologiae,* I, 18-4 *ad* 2
353 *Summa Theologiae,* I, 13-2; I, 15-2
355 *Summa Theologiae,* I, 93
357 *Physics,* II, Chapters 2, 8. *Poetics,* especially Chapters 4, 6, 9. V. E. Smith, *Philosophical Physics,* 49-58. *Summa Theologiae,* I, 117-1; I-II, 12-3
362 *On the Soul,* III, Chapter 4. *Summa Theologiae,* I, 89-5, 6 *ad* 3
365 *Contra Gentiles,* III, Chapters 19-21
366 *Contra Gentiles,* III, Chapter 49 (three ways of moving from effect to cause). *Summa Theologiae,* I, 6-1 *ad* 2
370 *Prior Analytics,* I, Chapter 6 (on syllogism). *Topics,* I, Chapter 7, and *Metaphysics,* X, Chapter 2, and V, Chapter 9, for meaning of *the same* and *the like*
372 *Summa Theologiae,* I, 93-9
373 *Rhetoric,* I, Chapter 11 near end

28

Material causality

375 *Principle of hylemorphism*: Every natural body is one substance composed of two incomplete substantial principles, related to each other as potency and act, and called prime matter and substantial form. *confer* 168, 255

376 Matter is for the sake of form. *confer* 8, 138, 172

377 Signate matter (matter marked by quantity) is the principle of individuation (that is, of individual or numerical differences) in natural things of the same species. *confer* 77 and Thomistic thesis 11

378 Whatever is received is received according to the nature or mode of being of the recipient subject. (Quidquid recipitur recipitur per modum recipientis.) *confer* 14, 169, 221, 363, 379
VARIANT   The cause is in the caused according to the mode of the caused. Note that this applies to form, model, and the likeness of the agent.

379 The material cause limits the form; the form is proportionate to the potency of which it is the form. *confer* 15, 169

380 Every change presupposes a subject or passive potency or "matter" which underlies the change and is found both in the term from which and the term to which of the change. *confer* 49

381 Since the relation of matter to form or of receiver to received is a relation of potency to act, every relation of potency to act in both the real and logical orders may be termed analogously a relation of matter to form. *confer* 260

375-81 REFERENCES

See also notes to *Form and Formal Cause* and *Hylemorphism*.

375 The description of prime matter in *Metaphysics*, VII, Chapter 3

377 *On Being and Essence* (Maurer edition), especially Chapters 2, 6. *Summa Theologiae*, I, 3-2 *ad* 2, 3; I, 85-2, 3; I, 86-1

378 *On Being and Essence*, Chapter 5. *Compendium of Theology*, I, Chapter 8. *Summa Theologiae*, I, 7-1; I, 7-4 *ad* 1; I, 75-5 *ad* 4. *Contra Gentiles*, I, Chapter 36

379 *Summa Theologiae*, I, 7-1, 2; III, 10-3 *ad* 1

380 *Metaphysics*, VIII, Chapter 1. *Summa Theologiae*, I, 75-5 *ad* 2

381 *On Being and Essence*, Chapter 2 (essential definitions), Chapter 4 (composition in angels)

Exercise 14
Material causality

"Whatever is received is received according to the nature or mode of being of the recipient subject." (378)

Directions: Indicate in these problems what influence the receiving subject has on the received. The references supply some leads to you. The key is on pages 146-47.

1 a being compounded of potency and act *confer* 14-16, 168
2 a being compounded of matter and form *confer* 375
3 seed and soil
4 the origin of new knowledge *confer* 303, 318
5 the importance of background in learning, estimating situations and people, correlating facts and principles
6 the patient's part in recovery of his health
7 the voluntary cooperation of the mentally disturbed with physicians

8 the capacities and limitations of various materials used by a competent artist *confer* 14-16, 169

9 the psychological characteristics of apperception, of projection, and of introjection *confer* 343

10 the original and the copy *confer* 350-51

11 the part played by prejudice in one's judgments of events and people

12 the limitations imposed by old age and weaknesses of the senses in regard to rapid learning

13 Why does bad example usually fail to scandalize the virtuous?

14 Why may individual differences validate the saying that one man's medicine is another man's poison?

15 In human acts which part plays the role of matter (recipient) and which the role of form: the act itself, or the intention; the experience that one has or the deliberate response to the experience?

16 A Why does Aristotle observe that the difficulty of learning first philosophy is not the obscurity of its subject matter, but the blindness of the student who is limited by sense origins of knowledge? *Metaphysics,* II, Chapter 1

   B Again, why does he think that young men are not apt students of ethics? *Nicomachaean Ethics,* I, Chapter 3

17 Why can only spiritual accidents belong to the human soul?

18 Participated existence is limited by the participating essence. *confer* 221

29

Moral order

Moral order in general (382-85)

382 The supreme end or good of man is the first principle of the practical order of human acts.

383 The general first principle of the natural law is founded on reality; and it may be formulated in one of these ways:

A Good is to be done and evil is to be avoided (as far as possible).

B Do the necessary good; avoid evil. *confer* 336

C The order of reality is good and is to be kept; disorder is to be avoided.

D Man must maintain right order (that is, the order of reason conformed to existential reality of man's nature and essential relationships). *confer* 230

384 Right order requires that means and everything equivalent to means be subordinated to and regulated by ends and higher orders of goods. *confer* 198

Hence, right order dictates priorities of A ends over means; B of wholes over parts; c of persons over things and authorities over subjects; D of higher over lower goods; E of higher laws (duties and rights) over lower ones.

A *In regard to ends and means,* right order requires that
1 means be subordinated to ends
2 proximate ends or means-ends be subordinated to ultimate ends
3 extrinsic ends be subordinated to intrinsic ends of the person's nature
4 pleasures, pains, and acts be subordinated to their natural purposes

B *In regard to wholes and parts or their equivalents,* right order requires that
1 parts be subordinated to the good of the whole person
2 appetites, desires, and emotions be subordinated to right reason
3 free use be conformable to and subordinated to natural end or function
4 social parts in as far as they are parts be subordinated to the social whole and its good

c *In regard to persons,* right order requires that
1 things be subordinated to persons
2 institutions, laws, customs, societies, and social powers be subordinated to the welfare of the members of society
3 creatures be subject to God
4 subjects be subordinate to their legitimate social superiors

D *In regard to types of goods,* right order requires that
1 merely useful and pleasurable goods be subordinated to necessary goods
2 less urgent advantages and needs be subordinated to urgent needs
3 material goods be subordinate to spiritual goods
4 private advantage be subordinate to the common good in the same order of goods
5 social and civic goods be subordinate to necessary personal and family goods

6 free, conventional, societies be subordinate to natural societies

7 created goods be subordinate to the Infinite Good

E *In regard to law, duties, and rights,* right order requires that

1 derived law be subordinate to more basic or higher law

2 affirmative duties be subordinate to negative duties

3 merely ethical duties be secondary to juridical duties (that is, to those binding in justice)

4 lower right be subordinate to higher right

NOTES A Since the principle includes the whole moral order, many other moral principles are merely partial principles contained less expressly within the range of the general principle of order. Examples are the principles on stewardship, on supremacy of the natural law among all laws, the frustration of nature, the subsidiarity of the state, the limits of property rights, and so on. B Disturbance of order must be removed and repaired. c Right order permits, without requiring, certain preferences: as a choice in the practice of affirmative duties, a preference of one's self to others in matters of equal needs, and so on.

385 Prudence forbids all acts, even the good and indifferent, which in the concrete would cause more harm than good.

Moral order in the care and use of one's being (386-91)

386 Man is God's steward or responsible caretaker of his life, his entire body and soul, and his property.

387 The Author of nature has made every natural power of man for its own proper good in relation to the whole man and the whole human good. He wills men to fulfill His intention in nature by directing the free use of these powers to their natural end or proper good and by avoiding use contrary to the natural good of the powers. Hence, persons have moral control of their powers, organs, and members only in reference to their natural ends. *confer 392-93*

388 A steward is required to use only ordinary means for the fulfillment of his duties. The measure of ordinariness in means weighs both the importance of the good to be cared for, the hardship of caring for it, and the evils resulting from less care.

389 *Stewardship of life:* Risk to life and even the indirect taking of life are morally justifiable for proportionate reasons. *confer 248*

390 *Principle of totality or stewardship of integrity* (especially of the body): A man may consent to a mutilation (excision, or temporary functional impairment) of a part of the body when the injury to that part is proportionately necessary for his life, health, or welfare. The proportional factors to be weighed are the risks involved in not making the sacrifice of that part, the good to be achieved by the sacrifice, the importance of the organ or function, and the immediacy of the need.

391 COROLLARY Any procedure directly or indirectly harmful to another is morally justified only insofar as it is designed to produce a proportionate good for the person harmed. Certain temporary and minor injuries may with consent of the patient be inflicted for the benefit of others in need. (Examples are blood transfusions, skin grafts, and so on.)

Stewardship in use of powers and organs (392-93)

392 Orderly use of the powers, organs, and passions requires that they be deliberately stimulated, exercised, or enjoyed only insofar as their natural ends can be obtained in such use.

Applications are to moderation in anger, in fear, temperance in food and drink, sexual indulgence, intellectual curiosity, taking recreation, and so on.

393 *Principle on the frustration of nature or natural function* (referred to as the rule of natural and unnatural *confer* 234D): It is contrary to nature and natural order if anyone intentionally uses any power or organ of his nature in such a way as to impede, prevent, or destroy that power or function in such use or if anyone so uses the power as to make it impossible or very difficult now or hereafter to achieve the principal natural purpose or good of that power or organ.

COROLLARIES A (This follows from 387, 392-93.) The general law of chastity: The primary natural purpose of sexual powers, the proper generation of children, can normally be realized only in lawful wedlock. Hence, the right to the deliberate use of generative powers and to the seeking and enjoyment of any venereal pleasures belongs only to the married in natural sexual relations with the lawful spouse; and such use and enjoyment is forbidden to all in any other situations. Note that this general law includes the particular precepts cited as—(1) Nulla copula sine prole: No intercourse preventive of offspring. (2) Nulla copula sine conjuge: No intercourse except with one's spouse. (3) Nulla proles sine copula: No offspring apart from intercourse.

B Application of the principle of frustration of nature to the protection of natural societies and institutions: Whatever makes it impossible or very difficult to attain the end of a natural society or natural institution is forbidden by the natural law and may not be sanctioned by human law. Note that it follows that no human lawgivers may legalize divorce, polygamy, birth-control clinics, sterilization of the innocent, interference with parental rights to educate, and so on.

Moral order of charity (394-98)

394 Every one must love God above all things with an intellectual love of both desire and benevolence.

395 Every one must love himself with a well-ordered love.

396 The natural law requires every man to love each and all of his fellow men as himself with a well-ordered love.
The measure of practical love required is mainly determined by the neighbor's needs. *confer* 384
VARIANT *The Golden Rule*: Do unto others as you would have them do to you.

397 Charity does not bind one to help one's neighbor at the cost of equal or greater harm to one's self.

398 Formal cooperation in another's evil-doing is never allowed. Material cooperation may be permitted under the conditions of the principle of the twofold effect. The circumstances of proportionate harm to one's self and to others if one does or does not cooperate, and the degree of immediacy and necessity of one's cooperation must be especially weighed in these applications of the principle of the twofold effect.
NOTE On the order of justice, see lists on *Property* and *Rights*.

382-98 REFERENCES

382 *Summa Theologiae*, I-II, 1-6; I-II, 71-6; I-II, 99-1; II-II, 23-3; II-II, 152-2

383 T. J. Higgins, S.J., *Man as Man*, No. 236. *Summa Theologiae*, I-II, 94-2

384 *Politics*, I, Chapter 5; VII, Chapters 1, 14. St. Augustine, *City of God*, XIX, Chapter 14. *Summa Theologiae*, I-II, 72-4; I-II, 92-1 *ad* 3; II-II, 19-11; II-II, 26; II-II, 152-2. *Contra Gentiles*, III, Chapters 22, 129. *Compendium of Theology*, I, Chapter 148. The most difficult point to express a rule about is the relation between the person and the common good. See J. Maritain, *The Person and the Common Good*, especially Chapter 4. J. Messner, *Social Ethics*, 113-14, 137-38, 194-95. Pope Pius XII, *On Human Unity (Summi Pontificatus)*, passages on the limits of state powers. H. Rommen, *The State in Catholic Thought*, especially Chapter 13, Section IX

386-88 *Man as Man,* Nos. 394, 401, 420. Pope Pius XI, *On Christian Marriage (Casti Connubii)*

389-91 Catholic Hospital Association, *Ethical and Religious Directives for Catholic Hospitals.* E. Healy, S.J., *Moral Guidance,* 156-64. *Man as Man,* Nos. 399-402. *On Christian Marriage* (passages on sterilization)

392 *Man as Man,* Chapter 11; the principles in his Nos. 374, 385, 300

393 *Man as Man,* Nos. 632, 726, 775-77. *Contra Gentiles,* III, Chapter 122

394-97 *Man as Man,* Nos. 354-63, 428-30, 659-62. *Summa Theologiae,* II-II, 25-1, 4, 5, 6, 8, 12; II-II, 26 (entire)

398 *Moral Guidance,* 43-47. *Man as Man,* Nos. 672-79

Exercise 15
Principles on stewardship

Directions: The exercise is based mainly on 388-93, but 385 on prudence and 248 on the twofold effect will also be helpful. The problems may be conveniently answered by selecting the letter or letters of the relevant principles. Remember that right answers require right principles as well as right knowledge of the facts involved. The key is on pages 147-48.

Possible answers:

A licit because it is a needed sacrifice of a part for the whole body

B licit because there is a proportionate good for the patient or person

C required as an ordinary means for the life or well-being of the person

D an extraordinary means; therefore, need not be used

E a licit means of helping one's neighbor

F licit for the sake of future protection against serious disease or other serious complications

G illicit because done without the person's consent

H illicit because of no proportionate good to the person who suffers the attack or operation

I illicit because it is a frustration of nature

J illicit because it is not a needed sacrifice for the good of the whole

K illicit because it is an evil means to either a good or evil intention

L illicit because the loss or risk is too great for so uncertain a need or method of treatment

Example: PROBLEM: The tourist, before taking a trip abroad, consents to take typhoid immunity shots. These, of course, give the patient a controlled case of typhoid fever. ANSWER: B, F.

Problems

1 When I am well, I give a blood transfusion to an injured man.

2 An ill father concealed his illness when he volunteered to give a transfusion for his very sick daughter.

3 M asks for anti-influenza shots from his physician, even though heretofore they seem to have done him more harm than good.

4 L with a serious case of allergy fever (hay fever) refuses to take immunity injections regularly even though he can easily afford them.

5 A mother insists on having the cornea of one of her eyes transplanted to her teen-age daughter who has been blinded in a flash explosion.

6 A professional boxer tries to win the fight by knocking out his rival.

7 The pitcher aimed at the batsman's head.

8 Though she knows that the dying patient is spiritually unprepared for death, the nurse drugs him into unconsciousness.

9 Unemployed and without means of livelihood from his savings, X refuses to take a proffered job because he lacks experience in that kind of work and fears it may harm his health.

10 A missioner, before departing to remote tropical regions where medical attention is scarce and unreliable, has his appendix removed even though he has no present symptoms of appendicitis.

11 The nun incurred permanent serious injury to her health in her efforts to lead a holy life.

12 The student rushing preparations for examinations stimulated himself with repeated doses of amphetamine.

13 A brain operation is performed on a psychotic patient as a first means of curing him.

14 A brain operation is performed on a psychotic patient with consent of relatives as a last means of curing him.

15 A heart patient refuses to moderate his work as his doctor had ordered.

16 Surgery to prevent the spread of cancer in generative organs also had the effect of preventing future motherhood.

17 After a third caesarean operation on his patient, the physician without the woman's knowledge sterilized her in order to prevent future pregnancy and a future need of operations and their risks.

18 A fugitive from justice has some of his features and fingerprints changed by plastic surgery in order to escape identification and capture.

19 Lacking any other drugs or anesthetics, survivors of a bad plane accident intoxicated themselves to help bear their pains and get some sleep while awaiting rescue.

20 The fertility specialist ordered the childless father to secure a sample of semen for testing by masturbation.

21 A captured spy slashed his tongue twice so that he would be unable to talk when examined and tried, for he was fearful of giving up secret information under torture.

22 In a polio outbreak in which not enough mechanical breathing aids were available, polio victim D volunteered to give up his aid to his friend, even though this might easily lead to his own death.

23 The actress takes monthly fertility pills lest pregnancy interrupt her dramatic career.

24 A patient with advanced cancer begs her doctor to discontinue X-ray treatments because they are too costly for her relatives to pay for.

25 Nazi officials ordered experiments on innocent Jewish prisoners in order to determine the point of survival and recovery after the body has borne extreme cold.

30

Rules on the names of God

399 The names that we give to God are first derived from our knowledge of sensible creatures. Hence, they must be corrected in meaning so that they will name God, not creatures.

400 No name may be given to God and to creatures in a univocal sense. *confer* 162, 460

401 No name that we give to God fully expresses His essence. *confer* 161

402 Any name that we give to God must be understood as proportionate to His essence, and hence must be understood to be substantial, subsistent, totally actual, absolutely pure, infinite, simple, eternal, unchangeable, and so on.

403 Though God is absolutely simple, we may apply many names to Him; and these names are not mere synonyms. But we must understand that each name, while presenting a perfection of God, excludes no other divine perfection.

404 Abstract names are given to God in a concrete meaning; but they specially signify the divine simplicity, and sometimes also signify that the adjectival name is possessed substantially and infinitely by God. Example: God is charity.

405 All names given to God must be understood in a substantial sense; none of them may be considered as adjectives or properties belonging to God.

406 All verbs and participles applied to God must be understood as applying to Him in a timeless, eternal, and changeless sense.

407 All relational names, expressing relations or changes in relations between God and creatures, must be so understood that in God no real relation to the creature exists and no real change occurs in Him because of the change of relationships between the creature and God.

408 Names drawn from creatures as the effects of God are applied to God as their cause, but not as though He had these perfections in any limited way.

409 Positive pure perfections are affirmed of God as actually and substantially possessing them, and not merely as being the cause of such pure perfections in creatures, and not merely as excluding their opposites from God's being. At the same time, even pure perfections named from creatures must be recognized as analogical names. *confer* 162

410 The excellence or eminence of God above all created perfections is expressed:

A by terms signifying His primacy (for example, *first* cause)

B by terms signifying His supremacy (for example, *supreme* good, *all*-wise)

C by employing repetition of the name (for example, holy, holy, holy Lord God of hosts)

D by using the abstract for the concrete (404)

E by stressing God's uniqueness in this perfection by the terms *only, alone* (for example, God *alone* is good)

F by explicit negation of limit or by explicit assertion of infinity (for example, *uncaused* cause, *infinite* truth)

411 Any name implying any imperfection may be given to God only in a metaphorical sense. Hence, anything material, potential, sensible, caused, limited, dependent, changeable, accidental, or relative is only metaphorically ascribed to God.

Suitable metaphors (for example, God's eyes, hands) follow no precise rule of propriety; but every metaphorical name must have a fairly obvious literal meaning and one that in given circumstances of culture and usage has no unworthy connotation.

412 Names implying evil may not be used even metaphorically of God.

413 It is better to say that creatures are like God than that He is like them. *confer* 371, 459

414 It is better to say that something cannot be done (because contradictory) than to say that God cannot do something or make something.

THEOLOGICAL NOTES A The internal relations between the three Divine Persons are properly ascribed. B The usage of the Church on the names of the Persons is to be followed. c The concrete names of the human nature of Christ may be ascribed to the Second Person of God since all predicates belong to the person, but they may not be ascribed to the divine nature.

399-414 REFERENCES

General references: Thomas de Vio Cajetan, O.P., *The Analogy of Names*, especially Chapter 10. G. Smith, S.J., *Natural Theology*, Chapter 11. F. Suarez, S.J., *Disputationes Metaphysicae*, Disp. XXX, 1. *Summa Theologiae*, I, 13; I, 5-1 (replies to objections). *Contra Gentiles*, I, Chapters 29-35, 89-96. *Power of God*, 7-4, 5, 6, 7. *Truth*, 2-1, 11. On the theandric names, see *Contra Gentiles*, IV, Chapter 39.

Exercise 16
Reading exercise on the names of God

Directions: Read St. Thomas Aquinas' *Summa Theologiae*, I, 13, to discover the problems involved in rightly naming God, and to find the citations of the rules which explain the meanings of the divine names.

31
Nature

On structure (415-20)

415 Every finite nature is a composite of potency and act. *confer* 158

416 The definition of all natural bodies must include matter and form. *confer* 167, 72

417 The forms of natural (material) things exist only in matter. *confer* 168

418 Form intrinsically specifies and distinguishes natures. *confer* 171-72

419 Every finite nature is really distinct from its powers and from the acts of these powers. *confer* 515

420 A nature, its powers, its specific acts, and its intrinsic ends and the formal objects of its powers are proportionate to each other. *confer* 132

On activity (421-23)

421 Every complete individual substance has a nature, that is, it can act. *confer* 39, 106, 511

422 Every nature acts according to its form. *confer* 87c

423 *Principle of uniform natural causality*: The same natural or necessary cause under the same adequate set of conditions always does the same thing and is directed to the same determined end. *confer* 107

VARIANTS A The same natural thing always does the same in the same way. B Like natures perform like functions and have like intrinsic ends.

On finality of natures (424-29)

424 Every nature is ordered to an end. *confer* 127

425 Every nature exists for the sake of its operation. *confer* 150

426 Each thing naturally and proportionately seeks its own being and perfection.

VARIANT Everything naturally aspires to being after its own manner. *confer* 182, 420

427 No natural desire is in vain, that is, purposeless, impossible, illusory, or deceptive. *confer* 35, 127

NOTE This may also be regarded as an application of 432 to desire or tendency.

428 The intrinsic end of all natures of the same species is the same. *confer* 146, 359

429 All nature is the work of the divine artist. Therefore, what nature intends, God intends. Furthermore, natural knowledge of God's will is learned from what God does in nature.

Axiological principles (430-34)

430 The order of nature (of the universe) is essentially good. *confer* 185

431 The universe is a realm of reason, law, and order.

432 Nature does nothing in vain.

VARIANT Everything natural has some purpose, meaning, and goodness. *confer* 127, 427

433 Nature is not lacking in necessities nor does it abound in superfluities. *confer* 292A and D

434 God treats all things according to their natures. Hence, He concurs with the action of all according to their natures.

Relation of natural to supernatural (435)

435 Grace presupposes, preserves, and perfects nature. *confer* 448

Knowledge of natures (436)

436 The mode of natural operations reveals the mode of a being's nature. *confer* 102, 108

Priority (437)

437 A Nature is prior to action.

B The nature of a thing is the first in each thing.

C Form is prior to formal effect.

NOTE On human nature as norm of moral conduct, see 230.

415-37 REFERENCES

420, 426 Many occurrences in St. Thomas' writings: for example, *Summa Theologiae*, I, 12-4; I, 75-6 (third paragraph, desire of immortality); I, 77-3, especially *ad* 1; I-II, 5-5; I-II, 62-1, 3; I-II, 91-4; I-II, 109-1, 5. *Contra Gentiles*, IV, Chapter 19

421 *Metaphysics*, V, Chapter 4. *Physics*, II, Chapter 9. *Contra Gentiles*, III, Chapters 69, 77

423 See 87. Also *Contra Gentiles*, III, Chapter 81 (arguments 4-6)

427 *Contra Gentiles*, III, Chapters 25, 44 (first argument), 48 (eleventh argument)

429 J. F. McCormick, S.J., *Natural Theology*, 253, 257-58. *Summa Theologiae*, I, 103-5 *ad* 2; I, 104-4; I-II, 12-5. *Contra Gentiles*, III, Chapter 100. Correlate with 434 below.

431 *Natural Theology*, 63-64, 234. *Summa Theologiae*, I, 98-1

432-33 *On the Soul*, III, Chapter 9. *On the Heavens*, II, Chapter 2. *Politics*, I, Chapters 2, 8. *Contra Gentiles*, III, Chapters 25, 48. *Summa Theologiae*, I-II, 5-5 *ad* 1

434 *Summa Theologiae*, I, 1-9; I, 43-7; I, 91-6; I-II, 10-4; I-II, 51-4 *ad* 1, 2. *Contra Gentiles*, I, Chapter 5; III, Chapters 1, 69, 71, 73, 100, 113

435 *Summa Theologiae*, I, 1-8; I, 60, 62; II-II, 10-10

32

Person

438 Person is the name of the noblest type of nature. (The bases for this nobility are the spiritual nature, the end in God, and supernatural elevation.)

439 The nature, its parts, powers, actions and passions, accidental attributes, merits and demerits belong to and are predicated of the person. *confer* 454, 515

440 It is a specific characteristic of persons to act formally (with conscious purpose) for their ends. *confer* 140

Rights of persons (441-45)

confer 482-87

441 Persons alone have rights.

442 The human person has natural rights antecedent to and superior to all positive law.

443 From the moment of conception every one must be considered to be a human person and to have all the natural rights of a person.

444 The rights of persons are equal where the natural or acquired title is equal; but unequal where the title is unequal. Therefore, all connatural rights arising from titles of human nature and destiny are equal; but they are (or may be) unequal where the titles arise from native and acquired differences in internal, external, and mixed goods. *confer* 374, 492

445 The being or substance of a person cannot be the object of any human right.

438-45 REFERENCES

438 The Holy Bible, Psalm 8. J. Maritain, *The Person and the Common Good.* J. Mouroux, *The Meaning of Man,* Chapter 6 and the conclusion, *"Res Sacra, Homo." Contra Gentiles,* III, Chapter 111. *Summa Theologiae,* I, 29-3; I, 93. United States Hierarchy, "The Dignity of Man," *Catholic Mind,* LII (January 1954), 123-28

439 *Summa Theologiae,* I, 75-4; I, 76-1; I, 77-1 *ad* 1, 3; I, 77-5 *ad* 1, 2; II-II, 58-2, c; III, 2-2; III, 35-1, 4

33
Philosophy

446 Wisdom is an architectonic science.
VARIANT It is the function of the wise to put things and knowledges in right order.

447 Wonder and the search for beatitude are the reasons for philosophizing.

448 Philosophy is formally distinct from as well as subordinate to the wisdom of Christian theology.
VARIANT Right reason
A is not religious faith
B is presupposed to genuine faith
C is elevated and supplemented by faith
D is subordinate to faith
E never conflicts with faith
F aids in understanding and defending faith *confer* 435

446-48 REFERENCES

446 *Metaphysics,* I, Chapters 1-2. E. Gilson, *Wisdom and Love in Saint Thomas Aquinas. Contra Gentiles,* I, Chapters 1-2. *Summa Theologiae,* I-II, 66-5

447 St. Augustine, *De Libero Arbitrio (On Free Will),* II, Chapter 9. St. Augustine, *City of God,* VIII, Chapter 8. E. Gilson, *Spirit of Mediaeval Philosophy,* Chapter 20

448 Pope Leo XIII, *On the Revival of Scholastic Philosophy (Aeterni Patris).* E. Gilson, *Reason and Revelation in the Middle Ages. Spirit of Mediaeval Philosophy,* 37, for the definition of Christian philosophy. V. McNabb, O.P., *The Catholic Church and Philosophy. Summa Theologiae,* I, 1-1, 3, 6

34

Predication

449 Names are given according to common usage.

450 The first known in a connected set or series often gives its name to other members of the set or series. The order of the names, then, follows the order of knowledge but not necessarily the order of reality. Thus, the accidents first known often become the name of the nature.

451 Causes are often named from their effects, essences from their properties, and the whole from its most important part or principle. *confer* 102, 294, 327-30

452 Change is denominated from its term. *confer* 56

453 Individuals may not be predicated of individuals, but other things, including universals, may be predicated of individuals.

454 Parts, powers, properties, acts, accidents, and passions are predicated of the subject (that is, of the substance, suppositum, whole, or person). *confer* 31, 439, 515

455 Powers are often substituted for the suppositum in naming the acting subject. Thus we say that "the intellect" thinks, rather than the man thinks by his intellect.

456 A known attribute of an attribute or part is also an attribute of the thing itself. *confer* 282

457 Opposite is not predicated of opposite.

458 The mode of predication follows the form and depends upon the mode of dependence of the predicate.

459 Things mutually alike may be said to be like each other. But things in different orders are not properly said to be like each other; but the inferior or dependent is said to be like the superior and the source, but not vice versa. *confer* 371, 413

460 No perfection may be predicated univocally of God and creatures. *confer* 162, 400

461 No perfection possessed by essentially different beings in essentially different degrees may be predicated univocally of these beings. *confer 222*

NOTE In cases of analogous names, the name primarily signifies the being or type of being in which the complete and literal nature that is named is found.

462 Universals are predicated of their subjects in a univocal sense.

463 Changes of names (extrinsic denomination) implies no intrinsic change in a being differently named because of such extrinsic relation. *confer 407*

464 Words are signs of ideas, and ideas are the intentional likenesses of things. Hence, words signify things through the conception of the intellect.

VARIANT Words describe the mode of being that things have in our knowledge and not directly the mode of being in the things.

Predication and truth (465-66)

465 In an affirmative proposition the predicate is always affirmed of its subject according to the whole of its comprehension and according to a part of its extension. In a negative proposition the predicate is always denied of its subject according to a part of its comprehension and according to the whole of its extension. When the predicate is a true definition, the comprehension and extension of subject and predicate are the same. *confer 533*

466 Restrictive incidental terms (and clauses) affect the truth of the proposition's principal term; explicative incidental terms do not affect the truth of the principal term.

NOTE According to 312 it is clear that the basis in reality for true affirmative predication is the real union of those things which are said of each other.

449-66 REFERENCES

450-51 *Summa Theologiae,* I, 13-1; I, 18-2; I, 29-1 *ad* 3; I, 77-6 *ad* 2. *Contra Gentiles,* I, Chapter 34

452 *Summa Theologiae,* I, 23-1 *ad* 3

453 *Prior Analytics,* I, Chapter 27

454 *Summa Theologiae,* many occurrences, for example, I, 4-7 (fifth reason); I, 13-12; I, 75-4 *ad* 2; I, 77-5 *ad* 1, 2; III, 16-4, 6, 7 *ad* 4; I, 25-1; I, 35-1, 4. *Truth,* 4-1

456 *Summa Theologiae,* I, 28-3. *Prior Analytics,* I, Chapters 1, 4

458 *Summa Theologiae,* I, 77-5

461 *Summa Theologiae,* I, 33-3
464 *On Interpretation,* Chapter 1. *Summa Theologiae,* I, 13-1, 9 *ad* 2. *Truth,* 2-2, c and *ad* 3
465 G. H. Joyce, S.J., *Principles of Logic,* Chapter 7, "The Import of Propositions," especially 105-06, the predicative view

35

Property

467 *Source of material goods*: God, the Creator of all material goods, has complete dominion over all these goods and all use of them. But He has not reserved this dominion to Himself.

468 *God's purpose in creating material goods*: The intention of God in creating material goods and the natural purpose of material goods is to supply the material means required for the bodily and spiritual needs and welfare of *all* men. (Nature first considers *all* men, and first considers their status as *consumers*.)

Means to accomplish this natural purpose (469-73)

469 *Use-right over goods*: Any man has a connatural right to use those material goods which are necessary for human life. This natural need of human nature gives him a title to:

A any needed goods not assumed by others as their own

B in serious need, the use even of goods already belonging to another if they can be obtained in no other way, unless their owner is in equal need of them

470 *Orderly distribution of goods*: The natural law requires men to manage material goods in such a way that the natural order of human dignity and of human need is considered for *all* men. Hence, in the interest of natural order:

A The natural law *commands* men to set up such economic institutions (1) as promote the effective and peaceful control, production, and supply of material goods for all men and (2) as maintain equitable access to goods.

B The natural law *forbids* (at least permanent) economic institutions which defeat or greatly hinder the normal purpose of the abundant, available, and continuous supply of material goods so as to satisfy human needs in a manner worthy of human dignity.

471 Orderly economic and politico-economic systems:

A The natural law permits and ordinarily commands the system of widely distributed *private ownership* of productive as well as consumers' goods and the widely distributed private control of such goods, under the guarantee and regulation of public law in the interest of all concerned with the economic process. Natural law especially protects the family's right to ownership.

B The natural law permits *public ownership* only so far as socially necessary or useful and not harmful to just private interest. *confer* 508

C The natural law forbids systems of highly concentrated private ownership or concentrated private control even without ownership. That is, it forbids a permanent system of *unlimited private capitalism.*

D The natural law forbids systems of *state socialism* under any guise or the permanent state ownership and control of all or the main capital productive goods and enterprises. It forbids political destruction of the system of widely distributed private ownership, as given in A.

472 *Acquisition of goods*: Every act of ownership, public or private, permanent or temporary, over any good, requires a just title. *confer* 490

473 *Restitution for injustice*: Every violation of just ownership is an injustice requiring restitution as far as possible. *confer* 384B

NOTE For contract, see 249.

467-73 REFERENCES

467-72 J. Cronin, *Catholic Social Principles,* Chapters 12, 5-6, and pages 88-93. T. J. Higgins, S.J., *Man as Man,* Chapter 17. Pope Leo XIII, *On the Condition of the Working Classes (Rerum Novarum).* J. Messner, *Social Ethics,* many sections, but especially 785-800. Pope Pius XI, *On the Reconstruction of the Social Order (Quadragesimo Anno). Summa Theologiae,* II-II, 64-1; II-II, 66; I-II, 105-2, c and replies. *Contra Gentiles,* III, Chapter 112 (sixth argument)

473 *Summa Theologiae,* II-II, 62

36
Relations and the relative

474 Relationship is the weakest of beings and the least of the differences between beings or principles of being.

475 Being is prior to relationship (to being related to another).
VARIANT The absolute is prior to the relative. *confer* 43, 479

476 Related things, insofar as related, exist simultaneously. *confer* 46-47

477 Related things, as related, are also known together.
Hence: A Related things as related are defined by each other. B Knowledge of one as related implies some indefinite knowledge at least of the correlative, and even definite knowledge if the relationship is equal. *confer* 286, 327, 329, 343, 366, 370-71

478 Wherever there is a principle, there is some relation of order present.

479 The relative is specified by the absolute to which it is essentially or of its nature ordered.
Applications will be found in the relations of accidents to their corresponding substance, of matter to form, of means to end, of parts to whole, of potency to act, of powers and operations to formal objects, and so on.

480 It is not the relationship but the relative thing that is referred to another thing.

481 Relative opposition connotes no imperfection.

474-81 REFERENCES
Categories, Chapter 7. *Metaphysics,* V, Chapter 15. *Summa Theologiae,* I, 28; I, 13-7, c and *ad* 6; I, 42-2 *ad* 2, 3, 4. *Contra Gentiles,* IV, Chapter 12

37
Rights

The holder of rights (482-86)

confer 441-44

482 Persons alone have rights.

483 Every human being from the moment of his conception has natural rights.

484 No one ever has a right to do a wrong.

485 Whoever has a right to an end has also the right to the necessary just means to accomplish that end. *confer* 134, 137, 565

486 The natural physical freedom to act connotes a moral right to act for the good, that is, to do anything not forbidden by natural law or by just positive law.

The object of rights (487-88)

487 The being or substance of a person is never the object of a human right.

488 To each his own. Suum cuique.
NOTE   The maxim applies most literally to commutative justice.
VARIANTS   A Let each have what is his own. B Render justice or his right to each. C Every right possessed by a person begets the duty in others to respect and grant his right to him.

Sources of rights (489-92)

489 Every right is based on a law.

490 Every actual concrete right is also based on a definite title.
NOTE   Application to property, 472; to contracts, 249.

491 Natural rights are prior to and are the basis of any positive rights.

492 Rights are equal where titles are equal, and especially where both titles and objects of title are equal. *confer* 374, 444

Limitation of rights (493-96)

493 Every right in the concrete and in its exercise is limited by:
A the purpose of the right
B the extent of its object, that is, by the title and the matter covered by the title

c our duties to others in matters relevant to the right; that is, by others' rights touching upon acts, objects, or effects of the exercise of one's rights   *confer* 488, variant c

494 Abuse of a right does not destroy right use or right of use before judicial sentence.

495 In a seeming conflict of rights, the juridically stronger right prevails. Some of the ways of determining the juridically stronger right are:
A A natural right prevails over a positive right.
B An indefeasible right prevails over a less necessary right.
c An inalienable right prevails over an alienable right.
D A right with a clear and certain title prevails over less well-founded rights.
E A right for more necessary, higher, and more general goods prevails over less urgent, less important, and private goods.
F A right based on a higher duty prevails over rights based on less serious duty or opportunity.
G In doubt, the right of the possessor is favored by law. *confer* 67, note I

496 In some conflicts of rights the juridically weaker right is not lost, but its exercise is temporarily suspended.

Defense of rights (497-500)

497 Force (might) may be used only in the defense of genuine right.

498 Persons and societies have the natural right to defend perfect rights against unjust assailants in proportion to both A the necessity of the measures necessary for effective defense, and B the comparative importance of the right or good under attack. *confer* 485
The law does not concede the right to intend evil, to use intrinsically evil means against the assailant, or to do more harm than good by exaggerated or useless defense. *confer* 234, 237, 385
VARIANT   Defense of one's rights is blameless when:
A they are unjustly attacked
B the attack is actual or imminent
c the right is one capable of effective defense
D the defense is the last resort to secure justice (that is, the use of force is necessary)
E the defense does not employ more force nor inflict greater injury than necessary for successful protection of rights

499 The right of self-defense is conceded to the person or society attacked, to one's helpers, and to public authorities as defenders of their subjects or of international justice. But while the primary holder of the right of self-defense is the party enduring the injustice, the primary exercise of the right belongs to public authority in organized society.

NOTE   The rights to kill another in self-defense, to strike, to wage war, to rebel, to punish criminals, are applications of 497-99.

500 A Retributive or vindicative justice after the cessation of the unjust attack belongs exclusively to public social authority.

B Authority in punishing must follow the twofold rule: No penalty without a crime; no penalty without a law.

482-500 REFERENCES

General treatments: T. J. Higgins, S.J., *Man as Man,* Chapter 15 and applications in other chapters to distributive justice, strikes, punishment, resistance to unlawful orders, war, and so on. Pope Leo XIII, *Human Liberty (Libertas Praestantissimum).* J. Messner, *Social Ethics,* 148-58, 187-89, 214, 220-32. National Catholic Welfare Conference, "Declaration on Human Rights," reprinted in many places, such as *National Catholic Almanac* and J. Eppstein (editor), *Code of International Ethics*

488 *Summa Theologiae,* I, 21-1 *ad* 3

497-99 *Summa Theologiae,* II-II, 64-2

Exercise 17
On rights

Directions: Indicate statements as C (correct) or X (incorrect) insofar as they agree or disagree with the principles on rights. The key is on page 148.

1 Only persons more than twenty-one years old have natural rights.

2 Even living unborn children have some natural rights.

3 All rights of all men are equal.

4 All connatural rights of all men are equal.

5 Any inequality in rights is unjust.

6 Men have only such civil rights as authority in the state grants them.

7 All rights arise, change, and cease chiefly according to the economic needs of the masses.

8 Men have some true rights which are inviolable by the police power of the state even in emergencies.

9 Might does not make right.

10 Might may never be used in defense of rights.

11 God is too wise and too good to leave men without the benefits of natural rights.

12 Natural rights are sufficient for men.

13 Positive rights are needed to protect many natural rights.

14 A right implies that I may do as I please with what is my own, regardless of the consequences. (Thus, I may kick my dog as I like or sell my inventions to my country's enemies.)

15 There is never a right to do a wrong.

16 Misusing and abusing one's right does not morally destroy that right except by way of judicial sentence for proven misuse or abuse.

17 The theory of limitations of rights implies a view of an order of justice in which liberty is regulated by fair laws.

18 Whatever is a legal right is also a moral right.

19 Whoever has a moral duty has a natural right to perform that duty.

20 It is never wrong to use one's rights.

21 Private authority may in self-defense *avenge* violations of rights.

22 The theory of forceful defense of important rights sometimes allows the killing of the unjust assailant against rights.

23 The person being injured, not the state, is the primary *defender* of violated personal rights.

24 There is no right to inflict a penalty without a law and a proved violation of that law.

25 Where nature gives a man a power or an opportunity and the laws of God and of man do not forbid one's action, there a man has a moral right to act. (For instance, the power to learn a foreign language, or to play a saxophone, or to trap butterflies in one's own garden.)

26 Animals who have long served their masters well have a right to be cared for in their old age.

27 Medical vivisection is a violation of the rights of animals.

28 Natural rights are all matters of justice.

29 "Laissez-faire" capitalism was wrong in its view of the unlimited rights of private ownership. (See also 470-71.)

30 The brotherhood of man requires that all rights, natural as well as civil, be equal.

38
Society and the state

501 God, the author of nature, is the author of the end, essential rights and authority, the essential duties and functions of a natural society.

502 A society is known to be natural from the capacities of human beings, their constant and universal tendency to unite in such a society, and especially their constant and general need for such a society. *confer* 143
NOTE See also under 129: The end specifies a society.

503 The state is a natural, permanent, and quasi-organic society having the twofold purpose of temporal peace (public justice) and public prosperity for all its members. These are the common good to be obtained by common means under law. *confer* 332
NOTE The common good is sometimes called the principle of public order and policy.

504 All sovereign political authority as such is from God and has natural right to obedience of the community in its just commands relative to its temporal social ends.
NOTE This does not mean that God designates each holder of sovereign authority.

505 All political authority is limited authority under God, responsible to the community, especially for its practice of distributive justice.

506 The state is a moral person, a subject of both natural and positive laws, and has moral ends, moral rights, and moral responsibilities.

507 *The constitutional principle* and principle of political prudence: The art of politics imitates nature. It must conform to the nature of men in society. *confer* 357

508 *The principle of subsidiarity or of subsidiary functions:*
A The family is prior to the state.
B The state exists for the good of all its members. Hence, it is bound to the impartial practice of distributive justice.
C The state has the right and duty to direct, aid, and supplement the activities of persons, families, and other social groups in

doing what is necessary or at least truly useful for the common good; but it is forbidden to usurp the functions of private persons and groups, and it may not destroy or impair any natural rights of association or of action by such persons and groups.

In other words, it may not act contrary to the common good, beyond the common good, or contrary to private good in matters which are sufficiently or better taken care of by private initiative and free efforts.

509 *The principle of pluralism*: Man's social nature rightly expresses itself in a number of societies, some of them naturally independent of the state and some of them subordinate to the state. Social order demands that persons be left free to associate in such groups whose particular functions do not conflict with the end of the state.

COROLLARY Hence, the state may not create a social monopoly, as though all social groups depended on it for their existence, rights, functions, and legality, and as though neither such groups nor the state could attain their ends unless they were dominated altogether by the state. In particular, the autonomy of families in their own goods and activities, of religious groups, of cultural groups, of vocational and economic groups, of groups engaged in health, charitable, and welfare services, of national minorities, of political parties, and of privately controlled communications services must be recognized and protected by the state. Hence, state monopolies destructive of or dangerous to such groups are forbidden.

NOTE For application to communism and nationalization of property, see 471.

510 *The Gelasian formulary on relations of Catholic Church and sovereign states*:

A Distinction; dual sovereignty: In the present historical order God has assigned supreme spiritual and supreme temporal power to two different authorities, each sovereign in its own sphere and not directly subordinate to the other. The Church can be only one; the sovereign states may be many.

B Scope of sovereignty: God has entrusted all divine and spiritual matters, in other words, all that concerns the worship of God and the salvation of souls, to the Church of Christ and her rulers. He has entrusted all purely temporal matters that pertain to public peace and general prosperity to the state and civil rulers. The sovereignty of each society extends to its own proper end, its authority, its essential means, its God-given rights, and its duties to its members. The members must be obedient to the authority of each society in matters pertaining to each in as far as they properly pertain to each.

c Relations of the two sovereignties in matters of common interest:

1 The Church and the state must both be interested in the welfare of their members who belong to both societies. Neither society can justify a policy of hostility, of non-cooperation, or of irrelation to the other society.

2 In mixed matters that touch the same members in both a spiritual and a temporal aspect, the higher end of the Church gives her priority of rights, but not exclusive rights. (Examples of such mixed matters affecting members in their ecclesiastical and their civil status are education, marriage laws, care of religious property, and so on.)

3 The Church, as religious and moral guide of her members, has directive moral power over their consciences in temporal matters insofar as such matters involve a religious or moral issue. The Church also has the duty to protect spiritual interests and prudently prevent spiritual harm that arises from temporal matters and temporal activities. Her title to such action is the salvation of souls as affected by temporal matters. But in the exercise of this indirect temporal power she may not use physical force nor may she intervene in indifferent and purely technical political matters.

NOTE Part of c is a later development of Pope St. Gelasius' statements.

501-10 REFERENCES

501 T. J. Higgins, S.J., *Man as Man,* Chapters 24-25. Pope Leo XIII, *Christian Constitution of States (Immortale Dei).* J. Messner, *Social Ethics,* 483-85, and so on. *Summa Theologiae,* I, 96-4. *On Kingship*

502 *Politics,* I, Chapter 2. *Man as Man,* Nos. 511, 699, 705, 738, 810, 815-17, 1123. *Social Ethics,* Book I, Part II, "The Nature of Society." *Contra Gentiles,* III, Chapter 85 (tenth argument)

503 *Social Ethics,* 275-76, 464-76, 486, 593-601. H. Rommen, *The State in Catholic Thought,* Chapters 13-14. *Summa Theologiae,* I-II, 96-1, 3; I-II, 100-2

504 Pope Leo XIII, *Chief Duties of Christians as Citizens (Sapientiae Christianae).* *Social Ethics,* 528-38

505 *Man as Man,* No. 307. *Social Ethics,* 193-94, 508-10

506 Pope Pius XI, *The Church in Germany (Mit brennender Sorge).* Pope Pius XII, *On Human Unity (Summi Pontificatus)*

507 *Social Ethics,* 112. *Expositio in I Politicorum,* Prologue, lect. 1. *In I Ethicorum,* lect. 2. *Summa Theologiae,* I, 60-5

508 J. Cronin, *Catholic Social Principles,* 77-79, 120-24, and Chapter 13. *Man as Man,* Nos. 821-22, 829-32, 841-42, 956, 977. *Social Ethics,* often given and in many applications, for example, 134-37, 196-99, 288-89, 302-03, 321-24, 573-79, 602-09, 735, 755-56, 805, 847-49, 922-27. Pope Pius XI, *On the Reconstruction of the Social Order (Quadragesimo Anno).* Pope Pius XI, *Christian Education of Youth (Divini Illius Magistri)*

509 *Catholic Social Principles,* 121-22, 216-20. *Man as Man,* Nos. 843-45 and Appendix I. *Social Ethics,* 138-42; 178-79; Book II, Part II, "The Lesser Groups"; and 390-93. *The State in Catholic Thought, passim* and especially 142-44, 354-58

510 C. Dawson, *Religion and the Modern State,* Chapter 8, "The Catholic Doctrine of the State." Pope St. Gelasius, "Epistolae VIII and XII" and "Tomus," in J. P. Migne, *Patrologia Latina,* Volume 59. *Christian Constitution of States (Immortale Dei). Christian Education of Youth (Divini Illius Magistri). Summa Theologiae,* II-II, 10-10. Pope Pius XII has a number of statements on the end, authority, and judicial functions of the Church: See T. L. Bouscaren, S.J., *Canon Law Digest: Supplement Through 1948,* 207-19, 231-41, 253-61, reported from *Acta Apostolicae Sedis,* Volumes 37-39.

39

Substance

511 Every complete being is an individual substance and an agent. (This is sometimes referred to as the *principle of substance.*) *confer* 39, 106, 421, 536

512 Every finite substance has only one act of existence and only one substantial form. *confer* 20, 165

513 Substance is not variable in degree *(stat in indivisibili).*

514 Finite substance has potency for contrary qualities, and so is accidentally changeable.

515 Finite substance is A the ultimate subject of inherence for all its accidents, B really distinct from its powers and accidents, and C the intrinsic source of its own proper accidents. *confer* 159 and Thomistic theses 5, 10

516 Accidents manifest the substance. *confer* 35, 294, 450

517 For direct human knowledge substance is an accidental (incidental, *per accidens*) sensible or intelligible object. (That is: material substance is directly known only through material accidents, one's own spiritual substance is perceived only in and through its accidents.)

518 Substance can come only from substance. *confer* 87

511-18 REFERENCES

513-14 *Categories*, Chapter 5

515 G. Klubertanz, S.J., *Philosophy of Human Nature*, 93-99. Sister Mary Dominica Mullen, *Essence and Operation in the Teaching of St. Thomas and in Some Modern Philosophies. Summa Theologiae*, I, 54-3; I, 77-1; I, 79-1; I, 80-2. *On Being and Essence*, Chapter 6. *On Spiritual Creatures*, 1-11

516 *Summa Theologiae*, I, 12-4; I, 87-1, 3. *Contra Gentiles*, II, Chapter 79, "Adhuc nulla res . . ."

517 *Summa Theologiae*, I, 86-1; I, 87-1; I, 88, *passim*

40
Syllogisms

Categorical syllogisms (519)

519 Rules for *correctness* of categorical syllogisms:

A A syllogism must contain three and only three propositions.

B A syllogism must contain three and only three terms.

C The middle term must be distributed in at least one premise.

D No term which was undistributed in the premises may be distributed in the conclusion.

E A valid conclusion cannot be drawn from two negative premises.

F If one premise is negative, the conclusion must be negative; and vice versa.

G No valid conclusion can be drawn from two particular premises.

H If one premise is particular, the conclusion must be particular.

NOTES Rules of structure (A, B); rules of quantity of terms (C, D); rules of quality of premises (E, F); rules of quantity of premises (G, H).

Conditional syllogisms (520-21)

(Formula: If . . . (not) . . . , then . . .)

520 Rules for *validity* of conditional syllogisms:

A When the minor affirms (posits) that the condition is verified, the conclusion must affirm (posit) that the consequent is verified.

B When the minor denies (sublates) that the consequent is so, the conclusion must deny (sublate) that the condition is so.

521 Rules for *truth* in conditional syllogisms:

A The connection of condition and consequent in the major must be true.

B The statement of the minor must be true.

Disjunctive syllogisms (522-23)

(Formula: Either . . . or . . . [. . . or . . .].)

522 Rules for *validity* of disjunctive syllogisms:

A When the minor affirms one member, the conclusion must deny the other member or members.

B When the minor denies one member or all but one member (if there are more than two members), the conclusion affirms the remaining member.

523 Rules for *truth* in disjunctive syllogisms:

A The major is a complete disjunction and there is complete (contradictory) opposition between the members in the major.

B The minor must be true.

Conjunctive syllogisms (524)

(Formula: Not both . . . and . . .)

524 Rule for *validity* of conjunctive syllogisms: When the minor affirms one member of contraries, the conclusion denies the other member.

VARIANT In a conjunctive syllogism the minor may not negate either member.

519-24 REFERENCES

519 *Prior Analytics,* I, Chapters 1, 4-7, 25-26. *Topics,* I, Chapter 18. G. H. Joyce, S.J., *Principles of Logic,* Chapter 11. For a versified statement of the rules, see C. Coppens, S.J., *Logic and Mental Philosophy,* 27.

520 *Principles of Logic,* Chapter 13

NOTE Rules on complex syllogisms have not been given here, as they are seldom used. E. Hugon, O.P., *Logica,* presents them. For axioms on inference especially related to the syllogism, see 287, 291, 293, 297.

41
Truth

Ontological truth (525-28)

525 The divine intellect is the measure of the truth of all things.

526 Conformity to the idea of the maker is the measure of the truth of all products (hence, of the truth of all the arts). *confer* 312

527 Everything is true insofar as it has the form proper to its nature.
VARIANT Every being is intelligible. *confer* 36

528 Being is prior to the true; the true is prior to the good. *confer* 44

Logical truth (529-32)

529 All truth is from God.

530 *Criterion of truth*: Things (forms) are the measure of the truth in the human mind. *confer* 312

531 Things are alike in their being and in their truth.
VARIANT There is the same disposition of things in their being and in their truth.
NOTE This axiom may also be understood of the material identity of being with its ontological truth.

532 Truth is one or self-consistent. A truth, whatever its source, never contradicts another truth. One truth may, however, complete the truth or partial viewpoint of another truth.
APPLICATION True philosophy, true science, true history, and true theology cannot be in conflict.

533 Rules on checking truth of propositions:
A For verifying the truth of a categorical proposition or an independent clause, examine the extension of the subject and the comprehension of the predicate in its relevance to that subject. *confer* 465
B Truth of conditional propositions. The dependence of the consequent upon the condition must be true. *confer* 521

534 *Truth in argument*: Rules on the relation of the truth in the premises and the truth in conclusions in a correctly drawn argument are the following:

A From a true antecedent in a correctly drawn (syllogistic) argument, only a true conclusion follows; a false consequent cannot follow.

VARIANT A valid conclusion from true premises must be true.

B Hence, if the conclusion is false, one or other premise must be false.

C From a false antecedent, either a true or false conclusion might follow.

VARIANTS From the false anything follows. Hence:

1 From a true conclusion one cannot infer the truth of the antecedent.

2 It does not follow that a proposition (doctrine, theory) is false because the arguments brought in its support are false. (There may be other arguments that have not been used.) From false premises we conclude "unproved," not "disproved."

3 It does not follow that the arguments used in support of a proposition (conclusion) are true because the proposition (doctrine, and so on) itself is true. That is, the truth of the premises must be judged independently of the truth of the conclusion.

D Whatever facts or truths are in accord with the antecedent are also in accord with the conclusion, but not vice versa.

E Whatever conflicts with the conclusion also conflicts with the antecedent, but not vice versa.

F From the contradictory of the conclusion, the contradictory of the antecedent may be drawn, but not vice versa.

NOTES A For rule of truth of definitions, 72. B For contrast of true and good in their existential status, 325 or 556.

525-34 REFERENCES

525-31 J. F. McCormick, S.J., *Scholastic Metaphysics*, 72-78. *Summa Theologiae*, I, 3-5 *ad* 2; I, 14-8; I, 16; I, 44-3; I-II, 93-1 *ad* 3. *Contra Gentiles*, I, Chapters 60-62. *Truth*, 1

530 G. B. Phelan, "Verum Sequitur Esse Rerum," *Medieval Studies*, I, 11-12. It has many texts. Pope Pius XII, statement on criterion of scientific truth in medical research, *Catholic Mind*, LIV (May 1956), 287-88

532 Pope Leo XIII, *The Restoration of Scholastic Philosophy (Aeterni Patris)*. *Summa Theologiae*, II-II, 1-3

534 *Prior Analytics*, II, Chapter 18. B. Pascal, *Pensées*, n. 394

Exercise 18
Truth in argument

Directions: Consider which rule of those given in 534 applies to the problem and how it bears on the problem. All statements, unless otherwise specially indicated, suppose a logically consistent syllogism or other valid form of reasoning. The key is on pages 148-50.

1 An error in the conclusion implies an error in the premises.
2 An argument that proves too much proves nothing.
3 Can there be gratis premises of a true conclusion?
4 Can there be gratis premises of a certain conclusion?
5 Whatever proves the major or minor also in turn aids the proof of the conclusion.
6 Though reasoning progresses from premises to conclusion, still a conclusion without satisfactory premises might be true, but is unproved.
7 Conclusions qualified as proved, disproved, or unproved are different from conclusions qualified as true or false.
8 It does not follow that a proposition is probable because the arguments brought forward in its support are probable.
9 Good causes and good doctrines may be damaged by false reasons. (For instance, pacifist arguments in favor of peace at any price may damage regard for the cause of just peace.)
10 Whatever disproves the major or minor disproves the conclusion.
11 Would an instance contradicting the major proposition make the conclusion drawn from it true or untrue?
12 Would a fact or instance contradicting a conclusion invalidate the premises from which that conclusion was drawn?
13 The consequences of an axiom can discredit an axiom. (Marx for instance argues that the right of private property necessarily leads to oppression of the poor.)
14 Can we immediately tell from an error in the conclusion which premise is false?
15 In rebuttal, which of these is the legitimate technique, which is the first technique to be adopted, and which is the better or stronger attack against the truth of the opposing position?
  A to point out inconsistencies in the reasoning
  B to attack the assumptions implied in the premises
  C to point out premises as doubtful, unproved, or false
  D to point out an error in the conclusion, independently of what the premises are

E after detecting and indicating an error in the conclusion, also to indicate error in the premises

F to attack an opponent's own corollaries from his conclusion

G to show undesirable or false consequences logically flowing from the opponent's conclusion

H to prove the contradictory of the opponent's conclusion

16 Webster in his reply to Hayne first attacked Hayne's conclusion, waiving the premises. Later in the speech he also attacked Hayne's premises. Was this technique desirable, useless, or moving from a stronger to a weaker method of refutation?

17 "Men can only deny one another's conclusions when they accept one another's axioms."—Eric Gill

18 If a bad tree cannot produce good fruit, how can an untrue syllogism produce a true conclusion?

19 Is it logically valid to judge, as is often done, a theory or doctrine by its good or bad effects?

20 It is often said that erroneous principles lead to divergent extremes and that error is endless in variety while truth is only one. Some instances are the theory of private interpretation of the Holy Bible leading to endless differences of opinion of the teaching of the Bible and endless variety of sects. Lying witnesses do not agree. Poor students in examinations give a fascinating variety of false answers to the same problem proposed to them.

21 Are scholastic philosophers atheists when they deny the arguments for the existence of God that are proposed by Kant or DeLammenais?

22 Why may we not argue from the justice of a cause or purpose to the justice of the means used in support of that purpose?

23 We will win because our cause is right. What is the connection between the elements of this enthymeme?

24 Many writers on epistemology refute skepticism as self-contradictory, impossible, and therefore false. They then proceed to refute idealism, relativism, and some other positions by "reducing" them to skepticism or to sharing in the fate of skepticism. What is the value of this method of refutation?

25 Could a person come to the conclusion that he ought to join the Catholic Church but give the wrong reason for this decision, for example, "because a gypsy told me to do so"?

26 Writers criticize Kant's theory of moral autonomy of the individual by these types of arguments: A his theory leads logically to all the excesses of individualism and liberalism; B his theory rests on the false premises of his view of synthetic a priori judgments; c his theory is wrong in itself because it destroys the very concept of obligation, law, and obedience by explaining law as the creation of man's own reason and will. Are all three methods of refutation valid? Which is preferable?

27 Can there be much truth in mental healing, even though not on the grounds alleged for such healing by Christian Scientists?

28 Can it happen that detectives may have apprehended the criminal by reasoning based on false clues?

29 Does the certain occurrence of one miracle invalidate the principle of natural determinism that physical laws are absolutely immutable?

30 Can the truth of Freudian psychoanalysis and other forms of psychoanalysis be judged from their results in helping some people? May we reason backward from their effects to their theoretical truth?

42
Unity

535 Being and unity correspond in kind.
VARIANT Everything has unity in the same way as it has being.

536 Every real being is singular, not universal. *confer* 39, 511

537 Every natural individual can have only one act of existence and only one substantial form as its substantial act. *confer* 20, 165, 256
VARIANTS A Ex duobus entibus actu non fit unum per se. B A thing has unity and being from the same source, namely, its act or form.
NOTES A The unit may have virtual multiplicity. B The natural unit does not exclude composition of principles of being nor real distinction of principles and parts within a being.

538 Unity is a measure of the perfection of a thing. *confer* 192, 218

539 The unity of order among many requires an intelligence as its sufficient reason. *confer* 134, corollary B; 138; 141

540 The natural unity of a suppositum is manifested by unity of activities for one intrinsic end, that is, by a unity of activities or by a unity of parts acting directly and primarily for the good of the whole.

535-40 REFERENCES
535 *Metaphysics*, X, Chapter 2. *Summa Theologiae*, I, 11-1, 5; I, 76-2 *ad* 2
536 *Categories*, Chapter 5. *Metaphysics*, I, Chapters 6, 9; VII, Chapters 13-14. *Summa Theologiae*, I, *passim* throughout Questions 84-85

537 A On unity of form: *Summa Theologiae*, I, 76-7. B On virtual multiplicity and virtual presence: P. Hoenen, S.J., *Cosmologia* (third edition), 280-300. G. Klubertanz, S.J., *Philosophy of Human Nature*, 21-33, 35-36. *Summa Theologiae*, I, 76-2, 3, 4, 6 *ad* 1. *Contra Gentiles*, III, Chapter 58; IV, Chapter 35

538 *Summa Theologiae*, I, 103-4. *Contra Gentiles*, I, Chapter 92, "Item. Quanto aliquid . . ."

540 *Philosophy of Human Nature*, 15-21, 33-34, 127, 147-49, 249, 298-301, 337 in which criteria and applications to human nature are given. *Summa Theologiae*, I, 58-2; I, 76-1, 2, 3, 4; III, 19-1. *Truth*, 8-8

43

Virtue in general

541 All virtues are really distinguished by their objectively distinct formal objects. *confer* 178

542 Virtues are living habits, capable of the growth and decline of finite immanent processes.

543 One virtue never excludes another. *confer* 208

544 Consequently, any conflict of virtues in a person indicates imperfection in the virtue.

545 (Moral) virtue is a mean between extremes. *confer* 191
VARIANTS A Virtue stands in the golden mean. B Prudence regulates the virtues.

546 There is no (moral) virtue without love of virtue.
VARIANTS A No one is unwillingly virtuous. B Charity is the form of all the virtues. *confer* 372
NOTE For particular virtues, consult *Index to Principles*.

541-46 REFERENCES

Nicomachaean Ethics, especially Book II. I. Cox, S.J., *Liberty, Its Use and Abuse*, 110-19. *Summa Theologiae*, especially I-II, Questions 55-56, 60, 63-65; II-II, 23-8. *The Virtues in General*

44

Whole and part

547 The whole is the end of the parts and hence their principle of unity, order, subordination, coordination, relation. *confer* 198ʜ, 384ʙ, 391, 540

548 The good of the whole is the good of the parts. *confer* 193, 196

549 The good of the part is reasonably sacrificed for the good of the whole. *confer* 384, 391

550 Every individual substance is a whole, with only one substantial form. *confer* 511-12
ɴᴏᴛᴇs   On distinction of the parts, see *Distinctions*. On predication of parts and whole, see 454.

547-50 ʀᴇғᴇʀᴇɴᴄᴇs
Contra Gentiles, III, Chapter 112. *Summa Theologiae,* I, 65-2, c (second paragraph); I-II, 92-1 *ad* 3

45

Will

Causality in the will (551-52)

551 No efficient cause other than God and the will itself can make the will act.

552 The will, in other words, is a first efficient cause in its own order of desire, choice, refusal, and so on.

Relation of will to intellect (553-57)

confer 323-26

553 Appetency follows knowledge.
ᴠᴀʀɪᴀɴᴛs   ᴀ Appetite is the natural complement of cognitive powers.   ʙ Nothing is desired or willed until known.
Note the following: ᴀ Sense appetite follows sense knowledge.   ʙ Rational appetite follows intellectual knowledge.

554 The appetible moves the appetite according to the way in which it is apprehended.

COROLLARY (combining 553 and 554) The will follows and depends upon the intellect.

555 The relation of acts of intellect to principles and conclusions is like the relation of the will to known end and known means.

COROLLARY Hence, acts of the will concerning ends precede acts concerning means. *confer* 569

556 Knowledge is of things in the measure in which their forms exist representatively in the intellect. Appetite tends to things as they exist in themselves. *confer* 325

VARIANTS A Knowing is intentional possession; willing is tendential possession. B Truth, the object of the intellect, is representatively in the intellect; good, the object of the will, is in things.

557 Intellectual knowledge is better than acts of will in regard to goods that are inferior to or equal to the knower's nature; it may be less excellent than acts of will in regard to nobler goods that are only analogically and imperfectly known by the intellect. *confer* 326

Objects of the will (558-60)

558 The intellectually known good, whether of end or of means, is the formal object of the will, and moves it as a final cause.

VARIANT The will acts according to the mode of its purpose, not according to the mode of its being. *confer* 233

559 The impossible, known to be outside our capacity and control, can be wished for but cannot be willed.

560 The first act of the will is necessary. Acts of the will concerning objects apprehended as naturally and altogether necessary are necessary acts.

Choice (561-66)

561 Choice concerns means, not ends imposed by nature. But the attainment of a natural end is often conditioned on one's choice of the right means to that end. *confer* 148-49

562 Only those goods or objects that are apprehended by the intellect as possible, as not necessary or as contingent, and as partial goods can be objects of free choice.

VARIANT Free acts of the will follow only objectively indifferent judgments.

563 Choice follows the ultimate practical judgment of the intellect; and it is the choosing which makes that judgment ultimate. *confer* Thomistic thesis 21

564 Who can will can refuse; who can refuse can will.

565 He who seriously intends an end also seriously wills the unique (necessary) means to that end. For example: God in willing the end of the universe wills the natural law for men and confers natural rights on them. *confer* 137

566 Summary of conditions for free activity of the will.
Principle: The action of the will is qualified and measured by our knowledge (553) and our estimated need of the object (554).
Conditions required for free acts are
A On the part of the object or motive:
  1 a particular, nonnecessary or contingent good
  2 a possible good
  3 an alternative good or course of action (since the good is particular)
  4 a means, not an end, imposed by nature
B On the part of the intellect:
  5 attention to the good or goods proposed
  6 deliberation between goods or motives proposed
  7 a contingent (objectively indifferent or mutable) judgment about the good proposed (This is a judgment of its non-necessity for the person choosing now.)
C On the part of the will:
  8 an act other than the first act of the will in a given series
  9 preference, consent, or choice

NOTE On moral aspects of choice, see especially 229, 241-47.

Priorities (567-69),

confer 557

567 The will is the primary appetite of man. *confer* 226, 114

568 Love is the primary act of an appetite in the orders of time, generation, and execution.

569 Acts of the appetite which are directly concerned with possessing an end are prior to and presupposed to all other appetitive acts. *confer* 555

General discussion: G. Klubertanz, S.J., *Philosophy of Human Nature*, Chapter 10

551-52 *Summa Theologiae*, I, 105-4; I-II, 9-6. These passages concern God's action on the will. For the denial of created action on the human will, see *Summa Theologiae*, I, 106-2; I, 111-2; I, 115-4.

553 *On the Soul*, II, Chapter 3. *Summa Theologiae*, I, 13-1; I, 19-1, 5; I, 80-2; I, 82-4. *Contra Gentiles*, IV, Chapter 19

554 *Summa Theologiae*, I-II, 9-1

555 *Nicomachaean Ethics*, VIII, Chapter 4. *Summa Theologiae*, I, 82-2; I, 83-4; I-II, 8-2; I-II, 9-3

556 *Summa Theologiae*, I, 16-1; I, 78-1 *ad* 3; I, 82-3. *Contra Gentiles*, IV, Chapter 19

557 *Summa Theologiae*, I, 82-3, 4 *ad* 1; II-II, 23-6 *ad* 1. *Contra Gentiles*, III, Chapter 26

558 *Contra Gentiles*, II, Chapter 35

560-66 *Nicomachaean Ethics*, III, Chapter 5. *Summa Theologiae*, I, 83; I-II, 13. *Contra Gentiles*, II, Chapter 46; IV, Chapters 95, 92-94

568 *Summa Theologiae*, I, 20; I-II, 27

569 *Summa Theologiae*, I, 20-1. J. Messner, *Social Ethics*, 39-41

Exercise 19
Will and human acts

A Complete these statements. The key is on page 151.

1 Rational appetite . . . and . . . the intellect.
2 Love is the . . . . . . of appetite in the orders of . . . , . . . , and . . .
3 The will is a . . . . . . cause of its own acts.
4 The . . . moves the appetite according to the way that it is . . .
5 As acts of intellect are related to principles and conclusions, so acts of will are related to . . . and . . .
6 The good moves the will as a . . . cause.
7 A human act must be . . .
8 A meritorious act must be . . . , . . . , . . . , pleasing to God, and accepted by God.

B Cite these principles and conditions.

9 the formal object of will
10 the conditions for freedom on the part of the object, of the intellect, and of the will
11 the extent of the influence of ignorance, of emotion, and of habit on the measure of freedom

C Correct these misstatements.

12 Choice concerns natural ends.

13 All acts of the intellect are superior to acts of the will.

14 All acts of the will are more excellent than acts of the intellect.

15 Natural ends are always attained by natures.

16 God cannot move the human will.

17 Willing is representative possession of the good.

18 Since willing depends on knowing, voluntary ignorance weakens willing.

19 Joy is the primary act of the will.

20 Choice is identical with the ultimate practical judgment of the intellect.

Exercise 20
Use of principles in natural theology

The key is on pages 151-52.

1 In which of the proofs for the existence of God are the following principles used?
   A the principle of sufficient reason
   B the principle of proportionate causality
   C the principle of motion
   D the principle of finality
   E the principle of participation

2 What criteria of real distinction may be applied to show that God is really distinct from the world?

3 How is the principle of limitation of act applied in proving the infinity of God?

4 Which of the axioms on knowledge do and do not apply to God's knowledge and way of knowing?

5 How is the principle of exemplarism used in discussing the providence of God?

6 What conditions for free choice are verified in God so that He must be said to be free in creating the world?

7 How is the doctrine of analogy of being and analogy between effect and cause applied in regard to the attributes of God?

8 What axiom or axioms on action and passion indicate that God can create without undergoing any change in Himself?

9 How are these principles used in discussing the possibility, actuality, and knowability of miracles?
   A the uniformity of nature
   B the principle of proportionate causality
   C the principle of evidence
   D grace perfects nature

10 What kinds of priority belong to God?

11 In how many senses is God a first principle?

12 Indicate ways in which the principle of proper causality appears in the fact that God alone is the Creator of all.

13 What limitations of human knowledge prevent us from a complete knowledge of God?

14 Which is nobler for men: to know God or to love Him?

Supplement 1

The twenty-four Thomistic theses

A number of popes and church law direct that the method, doctrines, and principles of St. Thomas Aquinas be taught in schools and especially in seminaries. After a special statement on this matter by Pope Pius X on June 29, 1914, a number of philosophy professors met, drew up a list of the principles and major tenets of St. Thomas, and submitted the list to the Sacred Congregation of Studies. On July 27, 1914, this Congregation declared that in their judgment this list contained the principles and major tenets of St. Thomas' philosophy, especially in metaphysics.

There was considerable anxiety whether this was a canon of orthodoxy in teaching philosophy and an implicit banning of views of St. Augustine or John Duns Scotus or Francis Suarez. Pope Benedict XV made it clear that the approval of the Congregation was not meant to close debate on these issues between divergent opinions of scholastic and Catholic philosophers. The Congregation itself, in 1916, declared that these were safe, directive norms.

Though the list often does not give the exact wording of St. Thomas, it is sure that the ideas are St. Thomas'. Hence, if St. Thomas is the safe, approved teacher of philosophy for Catholics, his ideas must be safe and approved norms. A philosopher who intellectually accepts all of these theses is named a Thomist; and this meaning of the term Thomist is about the only definite meaning that can be assigned to it.

The theses are given here for convenient reference. They are numbered 1 to 24 as in their source. They have not been numbered serially with other principles and axioms in this book for several reasons: they are often referred to by their own proper numbering in scholastic literature; they contain conclusions and sketches of proofs as well as principles; they range over many topics rather than concentrating on a single topic as the previous sections of this book have done. See especially act and potency, distinctions, efficient causality, hylemorphism, knowledge.

1 Potency and act are a complete division of being. Hence, whatever is must be either pure act or a unit composed of potency and act as its primary and intrinsic principles.

2 Because act is perfection, it is limited only by potency which is a capacity for perfection. Hence, a pure act in any order of being exists only as unlimited and unique; but wherever it (act) is finite and multiplied, there it unites in true composition with potency.

3 Therefore the one God exists in the absolute order of existence itself, as one and most simple. All other things which participate in being itself have a limited nature composed of two really distinct principles, namely essence and existence.

4 Being which gets its name from "to be" (existence) is not spoken of God and creatures univocally nor altogether equivocally, but analogically by an analogy both of attribution and of proportionality.

5 Furthermore, there is in every creature a real composition of the subsistent subject with added secondary forms or accidents. Now this composition would be unintelligible unless existence ("to be") were received in a distinct essence.

6 Besides the absolute accidents, there is also the relative or the "to another." Although being "to another" does not in its formal nature signify something inhering in another, yet it often has a cause in things, and therefore it has a real entity distinct from the subject (of the relation).

7 A spiritual creature is altogether simple in its essence. But there is a double composition in it: A of essence with existence; and B of substance with accidents.

8 But the bodily creature in its essence is composed of potency and act; these are potency and act in the order of essence, and are named matter and form.

9 Neither of these parts (matter and form in thesis 8) has a being of its own. Neither is produced by itself nor corrupted by itself. Neither is listed in the predicaments except by reduction (to substance) inasmuch as it is a substantial principle.

10 Although extension over integral parts is a property belonging to a corporeal nature, yet to be a substance and to be quantified are not the same in a body. Substance, considered merely in itself, is indivisible, not with the indivisibility of a point but with the indivisibility of something which is not in the order of dimensions (measurable extent). On the other hand, quantity which confers extension on a substance is really distinct from substance and is an accident in the strict meaning of that term.

11 Signate matter (matter marked by quantity) is the principle of individuation, that is, of numerical distinction, between one individual and another possessing the same specific nature. This is impossible among pure spirits.

12 Quantity is also the cause of the circumscriptive presence of a body in place. A body can be thus (circumscriptively) present in only one place, under all conditions of potency.

13 Bodies are of two types: living and nonliving. The substantial form of living things, called a soul, requires an organic disposition or heterogeneous parts in order that in the same being there may be a part that originates movement and a part immediately moved.

14 Souls of the vegetative and sentient classes are by no means subsistent in themselves nor are they produced in themselves. Such a soul is merely the principle by which a living being is and lives. Since such souls are totally dependent on matter, upon the decay of the composite they themselves are incidentally corrupted.

15 The human soul, on the other hand, subsists by itself. When a disposed subject can receive its infusion, then the soul is created by God; and it is naturally incorruptible and immortal.

16 The same rational soul is so united to the body that it is the one and only substantial form thereof. Because of it, a human being has the perfections of being a man, an animal, a living being, a body, a substance, and a being. The soul therefore confers upon man every essential grade of his perfection. Further, it communicates to the body its own act of existence.

17 Two classes of powers, the organic and the nonorganic, flow from the human soul by natural consequence. The first class, which includes the senses, belongs to the composite substance; the latter class belongs to the soul alone. The intellect therefore is a power (faculty) intrinsically independent of any organ.

18 Intellectuality is a necessary consequence of immateriality. Hence there is a direct proportion between the degrees of intellectuality and the degrees of separation (removal or distance) from matter. The adequate object of intellectual action is being in general. The proper (connatural) object of the human intellect in its present state of union (with the body) is contained in the essences abstracted from material conditions.

19 Hence, we receive our knowledge from sensible things. But since the sensible is not intelligible in act, we must admit, over and above the intellect that formally knows, a second active power in the soul which abstracts the intelligible species from the phantasms.

20 By means of these species we have a direct knowledge of the universals. Singulars we reach by sense as well as by the intellect when it turns toward the phantasms. We climb to knowledge of spiritual things by way of analogy.

21 The will follows, but does not precede, the intellect. The will necessarily desires that which is presented to it as in every respect good and satisfying to its appetite. But when more than one good is presented to its desire by a mutable judgment, it makes a free

choice. This choice follows upon the ultimate judgment; but it is the will that makes this judgment the ultimate one.

22 We have neither an immediate intuitive perception of the existence of God nor an a priori demonstration of this existence. But we do know of His existence by a posteriori demonstrations, namely, from the things that have been made, moving in our proofs from effects to their causes. These are:

A from things which are moved and cannot be the adequate principle of their motion—to the immovable first mover

B from the origin (process, emanation) of things in the world and of causes subordinate to each other—to the uncaused first cause

c from corruptible beings which are indifferently related to being and nonbeing—to the absolutely necessary being

D from things which have limited degrees of the perfections of being and of life and of intelligence and which have greater and less measure of being, life, and understanding—to Him who is supremely intelligent, supremely alive, supremely existing

E finally, from the order of the universe—to the separate intellect who ordained, arranged, and (now) directs them to their end

23 The divine essence, inasmuch as it is identified with the actuality of its own being, or in other words, precisely because it is subsistent being, is thus set before us in its so-called metaphysical essence. Thereby, too, the divine essence manifests to us the principle (root) of its infinite perfection.

24 Hence, by the very purity of His existence (being) God is set apart from all finite beings. Hence, we infer:

A first, that the world could proceed from God only by creation

B second, that the creative power whose direct and primary object is being as such, cannot be communicated to any finite nature, even miraculously

c finally, that no created agent can produce any effects in regard to being unless it receives a motion from the first cause

REFERENCES

Acta Apostolicae Sedis, VI (1914), 383-86, is the source of the list of theses. It evaluates them as a good statement of the principles and major views of St. Thomas' philosophy. The same *Acta,* VII (1916), 157-58, refers to them as safe, directive norms. *Acta Romana* (1917) contains a letter of Pope Benedict XV on interpreting the theses and on the measure of their binding force. *Ciencia*

Tomista, XV (May-June 1917), 381-90, contains a counter list of twenty-four Suarezian theses. Also see comment in R. Garrigou-Lagrange, O.P., *Reality,* 357-67, 343-46; in E. Hugon, O.P., *Les vingts-quatre thèses* (ninth edition); and in F. Pelster, S.J., "The Authority of St. Thomas in Catholic Schools and the Sacred Sciences," *Franciscan Studies,* XIII (1953), 1-26.

Exercise 21

Suggestions for study of the Thomistic theses

Teachings of the theses. The key is on pages 152-53.

1 Mark or underline the main topic of each of the theses.

2 Group the theses according to the way their topics fit into the branches of systematic scholasticism: metaphysics, philosophy of nature, philosophy of man, natural theology, and so on.

3 Does there seem to be any special reason for the order in which the theses are presented?

4 In the act-and-potency system, proposition 2 is the critical thesis. How does proposition 2 apply:

A to God

B to any creature

C to angels

D to matter-form composition, to composition of living things

E to substance-accidents composition

F to substance-powers composition

G to plurality of bodies of the same species

H to composition of changeable things

5 What are the exclusive prerogatives of the Being who is pure act?

6 What kinds of analogy are taught in the theses?

7 What principles cited elsewhere in this SUMMARY are included within these theses?

8 Study various contrasts presented in the theses:

A between potency (passive) and act

B between creature and God, both in being and in activities

C between simple and composite

D between matter and spirit

E between human soul and the vital principle of other things

F between human knowledge of sensible and of spiritual things

9 Evidence and proof of the theses. A Which are self-evident? B Which depend in whole or in part on the truth of theses earlier in the list? c Do any of the theses require independent proof?

10 What signs of real distinctions are implicit in the theses? What marks of essential distinctions are used?

Historical.

11 Which of the theses are Aristotelian in language? in doctrine?

12 Which of the theses are disputed by A St. Augustine, B Scotus, or C Suarez? Why so?

13 Are any of the theses defined Catholic doctrine?

14 Do the theses omit any important doctrines of St. Thomas?

15 Which of the theses are a safeguard against A pantheism, B agnosticism, C materialism, D dualism in regard to man's nature?

Supplement 2

Priority

This list brings together statements on priority occurring in the lists of principles. Few new axioms appear, but a summary may be helpful. The number following the citation refers to its earlier appearance in this book.

Being and the transcendentals

1 Being is prior to nonbeing. 40

2 Existence is the first of all acts. 41

3 Being is prior to the true. 44

4 The true is prior to the good. 528

5 The befitting or perfective good is prior in excellence and in meaning to the useful and the pleasant good. 190, 197, 384

6 Being is prior to change. 42

The proper modes of being and basic beings

7 Act is prior to potency in nature, excellence, and intelligibility. 2

8 Potency is prior to act in the order of material causality. 3

9 The unparticipated is prior to the participated. 219

10 The absolute is prior to the relative. 43, 475, 479
   VARIANTS AND APPLICATIONS A What is *per se* is prior to what is *per accidens*. B The unrestricted is prior to the qualified. C The perfect is prior to the imperfect in nature and efficient

causality. D Being is prior to relationship of being to being. E The one is prior to the many. F The measure is prior to the measured. G The object is naturally prior to the power moved by it. *confer* 13 and 15 below H If one takes away the posterior, the prior may remain. *confer* 47

11 Substance is prior to its accidents.
VARIANT The nature of a thing is the first in each thing. 437

The causes

12 Both agent, form, and powers have natural priority to action and effect. 98, 119, 171, 174

13 The agent is more noble than the patient. 92

14 The universal and nonunivocal cause is prior to a particular and univocal cause. 120

15 End is the first of causes.
VARIANTS A End is the first in intention, the last in execution. 122 B The mover is naturally prior to the moved.

16 End is prior to means and to result. 126, 123, 134

17 Means precede the end in the order of execution. 135

18 Form excels matter. 376

Knowledge and love

19 Knowledge precedes appetency. 323, 553

20 Knowledge excels love in objects inferior or equal to man. Love excels knowledge in regard to things nobler than man. 326

21 Speculative wisdom excels practical wisdom as an intellectual virtue.
VARIANT Wisdom is architectonic. 446

22 Love is the primary act of the appetite in the orders of time, generation, and execution. 569

23 Those acts of the appetite which are directly concerned with the possession (or acquisition) of an end are prior to and presupposed to all other appetitive acts. 555, 569

24 Some necessary act of the will must precede any free acts. 560

Order of discovery

25 The sensible is prior to the intelligible. 303

REFERENCES

General notions on priority and principles in *Categories,* Chapter 12. *Posterior Analytics,* I, Chapters 6, 10-11, 32; II, Chapter 19. *Metaphysics,* V, Chapter 11. *Summa Theologiae,* I, 82-3 *ad* 2; III, 1-5 *ad* 3; III, 1-6

10 *Physics,* VIII, Chapter 5, 257a 32. *Contra Gentiles,* II, Chapter 46 (fourth proof). *Truth,* 12-2

32 *Summa Theologiae,* I-II, 72-6

Supplement 3

Suggested list of basic principles

A student may wish to give special attention to the principles which are important not to some branch or topic in philosophy, but those which together mark scholastic philosophy as a distinctive type of thought. The major in philosophy may especially wish to be sure of his competent grasp of all the principles which seem to be the leading ones for explaining, proving, and correlating scholastic views. For such students the following list of about fifty principles is suggested, though there is room for difference of opinion in regard to adding to or subtracting from the list.

The principles are listed here by number in the order in which they occur in the book.

Act and potency: (1) act and potency, a complete division of being, 1; (2) limitation of act by potency, 14.

Being: (1) principle of contradiction, 33; (2) principle of sufficient reason, 35; (3) universal analogy of being, 37; (4) analogy of perfections of being, 38.

Change: principle of motion, 51.

Conscience: obedience to conscience, 63.

Distinctions: (1) criterion of essential superiority, 81; (2) criteria of real distinctions, 84.

Efficient causality: (1) principle of causality, 86; (2) activity follows existence, 97; (3) uniformity of nature (duplicate of 423), 107; (4) knowledge of cause through effects, 108.

End: (1) primacy of end among causes, 122; (2) principle of finality, 127; (3) proportion of end, nature, form, powers, acts, objects (duplicate of 420), 132; (4) relation of end to means, 134.

Evidence: principle of evidence, 155.

Finite and infinite: insufficiency of an infinite series, 163.

Form: functions of form, 171.

Good and evil: order among goods, 198.

Hierarchy: principle of participation, 219-20.

Hylemorphism: principle of hylemorphism, 255.

Supplement 4

Principles disputed among the scholastics

The lists of principles in this book have omitted comparatively minor principles upon which different streams in the scholastic tradition disagree. But some principles accepted by Thomists have been included, though these are not accepted by those favoring Augustinian, Scotist, or Suarezian points of view. It is only fair to the student to make some brief comment on principles which are in debate among the scholastic philosophers. The three main foci of these disputed points are A differences in the concept of being; B differences in the tests for real distinctions in being, and the substitution of formal or modal distinctions for real distinctions; and C the place of the will among the powers of man. Most of the positions of the scholastic nominalists have no support today and may be regarded as not belonging to a current divergence of view among scholastics. The several controversies on the basic one or more principles are not considered here.

Act and potency

The basic dispute concerns the limitation of act by potency in all instances of a limited act. Some claim that finite act can be self-limiting, because of its nature as act or because it is caused and dependent. From such a position it would follow that A in a finite being there is not always a real distinction between act and potency at each level or order of its being; B that not all finite beings are composite beings; C that act and potency are not principles of being, but beings; D that matter is imperfect act, not pure potency, and can exist and be created without form; E that finite act by reason of itself could be in potency to further perfection of its own order; and F that multiplicity is not always to be explained by multiple potencies.

Secondary disputes concern the unity or plurality of acts in the same being and the immediate modal union of potential and actual constituents of the same being.

Being

Some scholastics express concern about the universality of the principle of sufficient reason. They feel that this universality may impair freedom, and particularly the freedom of God. This fear, however, seems traceable to Leibnitz's use of the principle to support his optimism and necessary creation of the best world, though the principle itself does not imply a compelling motive for free action.

Universal analogy is challenged by Scotus because of his special notion of being which allows for logical univocity of being. The analogy of proportionality is minimized by some scholastics in favor of an analogy of attribution between God and creatures, and between finite substance and accidents.

The primacy of the act of existence is not pleasing to some who regard 41 as implying a real distinction of essence from existence or as prejudging the question of the quasi-metaphysical essence of God.

Finite and contingent beings do depend on the free will of God; some think that this dependence is the main or only reason for their finiteness and contingency, and thus they disregard the composition of such beings and the presence of potency in them.

Conscience

Instead of the principle of probabilism there are scholastics sponsoring the principles A of tutiorism: "In doubt always follow the safer course"; B of probabiliorism: "In doubt always follow the more probable course"; C of equiprobabilism: "One is free to follow a probable course only when it is equally probable as an alternative course"; D of compensationism: "One may follow a solidly probable course of action only when there is a sufficient reason for choosing it rather than a safer or more probable course."

Distinctions

Individuation or multiplicity of individuals within a species is ascribed by Scotus to the special formality of "thisness" or "haecceitas" added to the complete nature of the species; by Suarez to the whole concrete reality of a being or even of a part of a being (as a soul) which is thereby distinct from other beings of the same species. Numerical plurality of angels within a species is a corollary. Another result is a different view of the individual material thing as a direct object of intellectual perception.

Those who admit no real distinction between a substance and its powers will not accept a multiplication of powers according to their formal objects.

Of the criteria of real distinctions, only sections A, B, and F are universally accepted by all the scholastics. Criteria C and D have been interpreted as requiring only formal or modal distinctions, though admittedly they demand more than mental or logical distinction. Some of the others are accepted occasionally, but not in every instance. On this point, see *References* under 84.

Efficient causality

The one difficulty here is the use of the term "contingent" in the generalized formula of the principle of causality. The difficulty lies in the special use of the term by St. Thomas in his *Contra Gentiles*, II, Chapters 30-31. St. Thomas used the term only for a being which could change in existence or whose form was perishable. We tend today to refer the word to any being whose essence does not always require existence.

Finite and infinite

The dispute on axiom 158 is noted under "Act and potency," on page 130.

Differences in regard to axiom 159 are noted under "Substance," on pages 135-36.

In axiom 160, some would not allow the specifying phrase "as possessing potency." Otherwise, this axiom is commonly held.

Form and formal cause

Many non-Thomist scholastics admit the presence of actually multiple forms in the same individual. Among these one will be the chief form. Suarez does not admit such plurality in the special case of man. Hylesystematism is one of the substitutes among recent scholastics for hylemorphism. It is expounded in Bittle's *From Aether to Cosmos,* Chapter 14, and criticized in Brother B. Gerrity's *Nature, Knowledge, and God,* Chapter 7.

All the older scholastics admitted the real distinction of matter and substantial form. Dynamists deny the basic difference here.

Axiom 171 will be understood in a very limited sense by those who admit actual plurality of forms. In their view the highest form gives the specific determination and specific characteristics, but not all the characteristics to the being that is compounded of a set of forms.

Good and evil

Axiom 196. The precise statement of the relation of the good of the whole and of the part usually presents difficulty, especially in the case of persons, who are in one respect wholes and in another respect parts of society and of the universe. The rule is stated in greater detail in 198 and 384. One point that must be noted is that the good of the whole is not in opposition to the good of persons as parts of the social whole, but is rather complementary to their singular good.

Some few scholastics give some form of being to moral evil, though not to physical evil.

Hierarchy of being

Principle 216. The presence of all ranks of perfections is not due to a necessity on God's part. This is an inductive and not an a priori principle. Nonscholastics would omit the phrase on God's free choice.

Principle 219. The fear of Platonism seems to be responsible for many reservations in accepting this principle. Some hold it as only probable; some apply it only to exemplary causality; some apply it only to God and transcendental perfections. One result of these reservations is the frequent hesitation or silence about the fourth way of proving the existence of God from the grades of perfection.

Human acts

A number of different statements of the norm of morality are current among scholastic ethicians, though all these seem to be reducible to the same objective standard. The chief variant statement is the Aristotelian-Thomist dictum that right reason is the norm and measure of morality. But explanations of this rightness of reason show that it is measured by the objective nature of man as man. St. Thomas very clearly uses rational nature as the norm in *Contra Gentiles*, III, Chapter 129.

More important probably are the varying interpretations of the meaning of "complete human nature." Should this mean only the abstract man, the man of pure nature, or ought it mean the historical man, the truly complete objective man, wounded by original sin, rehabilitated by the Redemption, set in an historical and supernatural order? This writer inclines to the latter view.

The conditions of merit stated in 247 do not mention, but do not exclude, grace as essential. There is no purely natural merit from God. The phrase "pleasing to God and accepted by God" is known theologically to include supernatural aid from God and even the supernatural state of sanctifying grace for condign merit from God. Reason alone does not know the full meaning of the conditions for pleasing God. But ethical statements on merit which omit this factor are unrealistic and somewhat misleading. The man without sanctifying grace can do some good acts, but cannot merit beatitude by any of them.

Knowledge

Maxims 307 and 309 will be interpreted in a different sense by those who prefer to think that the divine being in itself and in its finite likenesses is the formal object of the intellect.

The debate upon the direct or indirect knowledge of material singular essences is omitted from the listed axioms on knowledge. Refer to "Distinctions," on pages 131-32.

Maxim 327 is opposed to the famous Augustinian view that the human soul is known in and through itself, by direct illumination and vision of the soul.

Moral order

No comment is given in 390 about the debated issues of the morality of organic transplantations from a still-living donor.

Names of God

If the names are not synonyms, what distinction exists between the divine attributes? The preferred view seems to be that it is a virtual distinction; but merely nominal as well as modal distinctions have also been proposed.

On a univocal use of the name *being,* see comments under "Being," on pages 130-31.

Suarez held that relational names could be predicated of God in such a way that a real relation existed between God and creatures. Now, this view also implies a different theory of the nature of relations than that expressed in the sixth Thomistic thesis.

Nature

All scholastics accept the wording of 434, though there are two important differences of interpretation. A The Scotist view holds that natural physical laws depend immediately on the free will of God, not on necessities intrinsic to their natures. This would seem to imply some difference in the meaning of the principle of the uniformity of nature. B The type of concurrence given by God, especially to free acts of creatures, is another famous difference of interpretation on the issue of God's treatment of

His creatures according to their natures. Bañez and his disciples stand for a premotion in one direction; Molina, Suarez, and others think that freedom implies on God's part a simultaneous and indifferent or multidirectional concurrence.

Rights

Axiom 487 has been worded to avoid the secondary disputes concerning the object of contracts of service and of work. What does the employer really secure a right to? Another's personal acts, the fruit of his work, a portion of the sales price of the objects produced, or some combination of these?

On defense of rights there is an ancient and unsettled debate whether physical evil against a person may be intended as a means to the moral good. Moral evil, of course, may never be intended. May the defendant intend to hurt the assailant or does he merely permit the hurt as accompanying the needed action of self-protection?

Society and the state

Scholastic views have consistently held that God is the ultimate source of civil power and sovereignty and that the welfare of all the subjects is the purpose of the state and the responsibility of its rulers. There have, however, from time to time been divergent opinions on the route of descent of power from God to the ruler, whether directly or indirectly via the community; and also whether this indirect route applies both to designation of the ruler and to the conferring of political power as such on him. The theory of responsibility *to* the community (as opposed to responsibility *for* the community) has also not always been held. The relics of the Aristotelian theory of natural slavery or natural incapacity to govern and to take political leadership have marred the clearness and fullness of the view of the community's primacy in organizing, delegating, and reforming government.

The theoretical position of church and state almost always tends to be clearer than the actual relations between the two societies. Today, of course, the state is actually in the ascendant in matters of joint interest.

Substance

On the unity of act and of form in substance, see comments under "Act and potency," on page 130, and under "Form and formal cause," on page 132.

On the relation of substance with its accidents: A Scotus tends to hold only a formal distinction between proper accidents and the soul or form; also that the powers of the soul are not mere accidents; and that the substance itself immediately acts. B Suarez holds that there is only a probable distinction between the soul or form and its proper accidents; that the distinction is modal rather than real; that the essence is to some extent an efficient (not merely a formal) cause of its proper accidents and powers; and that the substance acts immediately using the powers as its instruments. Along with these positions, there is a tendency in both of these schools to reduce the number of distinct powers in man, and especially to eliminate the real distinction between the agent and possible intellects.

All scholastics agree on a real distinction of the being from its changeable operations and newly acquired accidents.

Will

There is a celebrated difference of opinion, especially between Thomists and Scotists, about the relative superiority of intellect and will. The Scotists take the stand of the simple superiority of the will. A cognate view enlarges the scope of freedom of both God's will and of the human will; for in the Scotist view even the known necessary good can be loved freely. Hence, even ends can be chosen freely. Scotus maintains liberty under all conditions of the judgment of the intellect. Suarez maintains liberty independently of the ultimate practical judgment. For Suarez all that is prerequisite is a judgment that the object is capable of being chosen.

If the will is the supreme power, then the meaning or application of 144 and 148 will be rather different. So, the Thomists place human beatitude formally in the intellect; the Scotists place it formally in the will. Thus, the roles of knowledge and of love in life both on earth and in heaven are differently weighted by these schools.

Answers to exercises

Exercise 1, pages 8-9
Recognizing principles

1 real, material cause
2 logical; problem, sign
3 real, cause
4 real, occasion
5 real; beginning, integral part
6 logical, standard of measurement
7 real, formal cause
8 real, occasion (or condition)
9 logical, sign
10 real, occasion
11 real, purpose
12 real, purpose
13 logical, truth as a starting point
14 real, condition (purpose)
15 logical, standard
16 real, cause
17 real, occasion
18 real, purpose
19 real, cause and standard or model

20 logical, sign
21 real, cause
22 logical, starting point of knowledge
23 real, material cause
24 real, material cause
25 real, foundation
26 real, occasion
27 real, purpose
28 logical, standard
29 real, agent
30 real, formal cause
31 real, condition
32 logical, sign
33 real, purpose
34 real, occasion
35 real, condition
36 logical, sign
37 logical, general truth
38 real, exemplar

Exercise 2, page 17
Some uses of the principle of sufficient reason

A Clues are given in the principles referred to.

B 1 the activity of an efficient cause, 86, and receptivity in the material cause, 49
2 the creative act of a necessary being, 86, 163
3 the wise choice of God; many finite exemplars to imitate the infinite excellence of God; variety of forms; *confer* 75-76, 216, 218, 352
4 divine intelligence, 139, 141, 539
5 finiteness of things; and God's permission for the sake of good; 200-01
6 the support of the substance as substratum in which the accidents inhere
7 the vital principle or soul, 258
8 the unity of the soul, 20, 537
9 spirituality of the soul; need for beatitude and sanctions
10 objective evidence presented to infallible knowing powers, 155

11 likeness to their maker's intelligence, 369, 526
12 the eternal law
13 means given by God because men need them to obtain their necessary end and to observe natural law, 137, 485, 565
14 the dignity of human personality; God's government for men's own welfare
15 the limited and merely temporal end of the state and its subsidiary character, 503-05, 508, 510

Exercise 3, pages 22-23
Principles concerning conscience

1 The father acts without a certain conscience in a matter in which he is bound to protect his child against probable harm.
2 Strong suspicion is not moral certainty. The right of the student is involved. *confer* 66 There at most would be a right on the instructor's part to request a reasonable re-examination.
3 The American man's doubt concerns a necessary end, namely, his own moral welfare and salvation. He must wait until he is morally sure.
4 The policeman's act may be condoned if he reports that this *may* have been the number of the license plate, and therefore may deserve investigation. If he reports without this reservation, he acts in a doubt that may lead to harm to an innocent driver.
5 In this case the pharmacist seems to have taken sufficient means to protect the customer.
6 The doubt of law must be cleared before the tax can be justly assessed. See also 337D and 339.
7 The juror should rest his judgment on the evidence, not on the opinions of the other jurors. Hence, he must vote "not guilty."
8 The politician is acting in practical doubt and is risking harm to his auditors as a means to his own popularity. The argument about the harmless results of similar jokes in plays, and so on, is surely not a certain argument. See also 248 on the twofold effect.
9 If the doctor knows that his recommendation may have any favorable or unfavorable force with the admissions committee, he ought to decline the request to give an opinion on the applicant's qualifications.
10 This is ignorance of a vincible and voluntary kind. See also 242.
11 Unless there is an emergency that demands her instant action, her act is not justified. It is another question whether she is responsible for late-coming and for being an indirect probable cause of danger to patients.
12 He must inquire until his doubt is solved. Of course, prayer to know the will of God in the matter is also needed. He has no obligation to give up his Hebrew religion until he is morally sure that such a course is God's will.

13 This is acting in vincible ignorance and practical doubt that exposes the daughter to great risks without any compensating reasons.

14 The argument about exaggerated criticism has no basis, as far as stated in the case. Hence, it does not solve their doubt. They must take other better steps to solve the doubt before they may attend the picture.

Exercise 4, pages 27-28
Identifying essential superiority

  1 immanent acts of various kinds

  2 conscious acts, including sensory knowledge and sensitive desires, for they show freedom from the restrictions of mere matter and material change

  3 acts of nutrition, growth, self-repair, reproduction, adaptation, self-organization

  4 spiritual nature of thought shown by its objects: universals and transcendentals, the simple and spiritual, the mediate or unseen, the future, meanings and relationships; perception of the self, judgment, reasoning, use of language with understanding of it

  5 spiritual nature of objects of volition: God, the morally good, and so on; freedom in some acts of will

  6 activities of intellect and will as in 4 and 5 above, showing spirituality

  7 immanent activity; spiritual activity; immortality

  8 no dependence even extrinsic on bodies for their knowledge, condition of being or well-being; no union with matter, and so not limited by space, place, time, condition of matter

  9 capacity for love of God, for merit with God, for vision of God in the next life; godlike life

10 Trees show only complex variations of the basic activities possessed by grass.

11 Each has the same powers, the same types of activities, and, hence, the same human nature. *confer* 146, 444, 461-62

Exercise 5, pages 28-29
Identifying real distinctions by use of criteria

The clues are given in the exercise itself. Specific additional information on the philosophical questions in the minor premises, if such be needed, will be obtained by consulting some philosophical study of the particular topic or by referring to the index of this book, as under "Hylemorphism," "Vitalism," "Act and potency," and so on.

Exercise 6, pages 35-36
Citation of principles on efficient causality

A 1 really, 45
    2 knowledge, existence, power, nature, 96, 108
    3 cannot, itself, 91
    4 necessary, 111
    5 no secondary, 89
    6 God, the first cause, 104F
    7 principal, immediate, living, 117

B Scan the principles in the text to check on your memory of them.

C 1 Number 86   The word *effect* makes this statement tautological, not a principle.
    2 Number 96
    3 Number 47
    4 Numbers 46, 52   *Simultaneous* is the key.
    5 Number 87B   *Virtually* is the key.
    6 Number 108   *Completely* is an exaggerated description of the likeness leading to the knowledge.
    7 Numbers 118, 62
    8 Number 47, the last phrase

Exercise 7, page 36
Action follows existence

  1 Any immanent or self-perfecting acts, as nourishment, growth, sensation, emotion, reasoning, and so on.
  2 Spiders spinning webs, birds building nests and hatching eggs, the migration of birds, bees forming honeycombs, and so on, show actions concerned with the good of the individual and species, which are specific, uniform in the species, and unlearned.
  3 Coordinated acts for the good of the whole man, as movement of the body when a dangerous object is sighted coming toward one; the act of command to perform a desired act with the help of the whole person's powers; the knowledge of the unity of one's person in spite of its many different acts and experiences. *confer* 540
  4 By the immateriality of the objects known: as universal, spiritual objects which are thought about, future objects, understanding meanings and logical relationships, and so on. *confer* 178
  5 The complete dependence on the existence, attention, and action of the physical organ. If it is excised, drugged, or impeded from action, no sensation occurs.

6 See 204. Operative habits are referred to in the problem. Regularity, facility, and pleasure are experienced in our activities such as speaking English correctly, devout attention in praying, neatness of appearance, setting an alarm clock, and so on.

7 The acts that show spirituality of the intellect; also, the acts that show freedom of the will and desire for spiritual goods as the love of God and of virtues. *confer* Exercise 4, answer 4

8 The act of thinking of simple (indivisible) objects; the act of self-awareness and self-reflection.

9 See replies to Exercise 4, answers 7-8.

10 The health and activity of the senses aid knowledge; their handicaps, fatigue, injury, weakening in age, limit knowledge.

11 Acts of choice, consent, resistance, rejection; also, the acts of deliberation and the sense of guilt since these require a sufficient reason in our knowledge of our power to choose rightly or wrongly.

12 Changes from illness to health, from rest to fatigue, and in attention to one object after another; changes of bodily position; growth in knowledge and in virtue; changes from silence to speech. All these occur in the same ego who remains substantially the same.

13 Acts of choice and of planning and of perseverance until goals are finally achieved.

14 Acts of memory in which one now recognizes the ego to be the same as in years long past.

15 See any good text in introduction to general psychology or in tests and measurements. Ability is rated by specific acts that indicate intellectual capacity, or mechanical ability or moral judgments and choices, and so on.

Exercise 8, page 37
Uses of principles on efficient causality

1 Numbers 87A, 87C, 95A
2 Numbers 107, 111
3 Numbers 86-87, 104
4 Number 96
5 Number 108
6 Number 86
7 Number 99
8 Numbers 86, 88, 141
9 Numbers 87, 98, 104 (absence of proximate cause), 107
10 Number 47
11 Number 104C
12 Numbers 95, 100
13 Numbers 87, 104B
14 Numbers 87C, 95A, 100
15 Number 47
16 Number 87B
17 Numbers 87, 112
18 Numbers 97, 102
19 Number 108
20 Number 102

Exercise 9, page 42
Citation of principles on end

A 1 Number 123
   2 Number 127 under variants
   3 Number 140

   4 Numbers 136, 47
   5 Numbers 134, 540, 547
   6 Number 129

B Scan the principles in the text to test your identification of the principles and exact expression of them.

C 1 Number 145   This also disregards organic unity, 540.
   2 Number 122
   3 Number 149

   4 Number 140c
   5 Number 124
   6 Number 151

Exercise 10, *pages* 42-43
Uses of principles on final cause

   1 Numbers 134, corollary B; 137; 125
   2 Numbers 124, 141 (Heaven is the perfect state, and God rules it.)
   3 Numbers 139, 140A, 141
   4 Numbers 35, 127
   5 Numbers 127, 134, 136
   6 Number 134
   7 Numbers 152, 418, 429

   8 Numbers 127, 122, 129
   9 Numbers 137, 335
   10 Numbers 127, 134, 332
   11 Numbers 134, 332
   12 Number 143
   13 Numbers 145; 134, corollaries A and B; 390; 547-49
   14 Number 144
   15 Numbers 137, 134, 132
   16 Number 134, corollary D

Exercise 11, *pages* 47-48
Formal objects

A 1 intelligible species (abstracted from phantasms)
   2 actual color (a surface emitting light into the eye)
   3 sound
   4 flavor
   5 image of absent sensible objects
   6 circulation of blood
   7 act of external senses and common object of different sensations
   8 sensible (pleasurable) good
   9 relative warmth of bodies
   10 the living body, especially its preservation in life
   11 arduous sensible good
   12 being
   13 intellectually apprehended good

B 1 things to be made
   2 first principles
   3 being as being (or as absolutely first principles; or, immaterial being)
      But note that this answer is disputed and also that there is more than
      one meaning to "being as being."
   4 obligatory good
   5 changeable being
   6 things to be done (right means)
   7 structure (of plants, animals, human body)
   8 function of organs
   9 plants
   10 animals
   11 health
   12 speech honoring God
   13 authority of God revealing
   14 rights due to others
   15 exact right due to one's equal
   16 difficult good (to be chosen and done)
   17 difficult means to a possible but uncertain end
   18 honor due to God
   19 truth
   20 first principles of natural law
   21 first principles of common good
   22 means of government organization and functioning
   23 movement of ships
   24 action of noble characters against willful and overpowering evil

C 1 Both have the same formal object.
   2 Sense memory retains and recalls sense images. Hence, it is one function
      of the imagination.
   3 See 179, second sentence.
   4 See 179, second sentence.

D 1 Speech combines several powers into a unified action, as the will, intel-
      lect, memory of symbols, kinesthetic sensory power (touch), motor con-
      trol of vocal cords, and so on. But it has no distinct object of its own.
      Speech as a habit may be said to have a distinct object.
   2 Pain is experienced by all the senses, not just by some special one.
   3 Melody is a sequence of sounds. It may involve memory as well as
      hearing, but is not a new formal object.
   4 Kinesthetic sensations may have as their object pressure, resistances,
      stresses of muscles, tendons, and so on, within the body. Hence, they
      are only accidentally different in object from pressures and resistances
      of objects external to the body.

The principle of economy

1 Plants give no evidence of sensory knowledge. There is no need of sensation to explain any of the vital activities of plants. Many of them lack the organic structure which sensation shows as needed in animals. Finally, sensation would be harmful to many plants rather than being a perfection of their natures. *confer* 427, 432

2 All phenomena of animal learning and knowledge can be explained without intelligence on the part of the animal. There are quite clear signs that animals lack intelligence; and they give no sure signs of intelligence such as the use of meaningful language.

3 There is no evidence of innate ideas, and there is no need of them to explain human knowledge. The marks of sensory origin seem to be on all or nearly all our knowledge. But the theory of innate ideas is not contradictory.

4 The asserted plurality of souls is useless, since actual unity with several functions or merely virtual plurality sufficiently explains the various levels of human living activity. *confer* 292A and B There is immense evidence for substantial unity in man. See also the principle of vitalism and unity of act.

5 Spirit cannot evolve from matter or from spirit. Hence, since it exists newly, it must originate by creation. See also answer to 16 below.

6 There is no need of this hypothesis to explain human life, human knowledge, or human destiny. Pre-existence would be purposeless existence. Hence, it is a gratis though not a contradictory postulate.

7 There is no way of disproving some natural ability for extrasensory perception; and there is some favorable evidence for such knowledge at a distance between acutely sympathetic persons. It somewhat resembles angelic communication.

8 Abnormal and hysterical conditions can cause such unusual physical phenomena. Where there is lack of signs of genuine sanctity, lack of special spiritual purpose, or signs of doubtful mental balance and control in the stigmatic, the wounds are not to be considered miraculous or supernatural in character. *confer* 292c

9 Number 292A

10 Number 291

11 Number 292B   Mental cures, gradual cures, minor improvements, temporary improvements, and so on, do not give sufficient evidence that nature cannot accomplish them.

12 Number 292D   The one law sufficiently explains the many varieties of motion, direction, acceleration, and force which it is designed to put into orderly relation.

13 Present knowledge of genetics and embryonic development show that the human being is specifically human in being and trend of development right from the start. The previous postulate based on too little knowledge of prenatal development is not needed and has no argument in its support.

14 There is a proportionate material cause for sensation, a material reality. But intellectual knowledge is a spiritual activity, for which sensible objects and sensible images are an insufficient cause.

15 Space can be sufficiently explained as a being of reason, obtained by abstraction from the quantity of bodies and conceived of as a container of bodies.

16 All other explanations are insufficient or contradictory. The only alternative is origin from nothingness by divine power; and this does explain origin of a contingent and diversified universe.

17 The fact of creation and the time of creation or of the duration of creation are two different issues. St. Thomas felt that there was no evidence of fact, of necessity, or of impossibility available to reason to settle the latter question of creation in eternity or in time. He admitted, of course, the revealed teaching of creation in time.

18 A The strict substantial simplicity of God forbids all plurality.

B There are two different ways of thinking of God, as being and as cause. But these are not two different realities in the all-simple nature of God.

C Immortality is not a power, habit, or other accident. It is a description of the kind of life that the soul naturally has.

D Rationality (not intellectuality) implies dependence on a sensitive organism. An essential definition does not give the distinct physical parts of a being, but gives genus and specific difference.

E See 27-29. The same reality is action when considered as proceeding from the cause or as related to the cause; it is passion when considered as in the patient or as related to the effect.

19 Natural rights are deduced by an argument based on their necessity for human destiny and human welfare. Hence, the principle of economy is used. Other rights are based on positive law, on custom, or on a broad meaning of the word right as equivalent to a natural interest.

20 Without benefit of microscopic knowledge of life and of bacteria, St. Thomas noted the fact of the origin of insect life from decaying and dead matter. So, he postulated an adequate cause in the heavenly bodies. Pasteur discovered bacterial life and found that life always came from life already existent in this supposedly dead matter.

21 A Will and free will both have the same object, the intellectually apprehended good. Free will needs the added condition of a nonnecessary good and a contingent judgment about such a good; but it does not need a different formal object than intellectual appetite needs.

B Imagination retains, recalls, and reassembles images of absent objects. Hence, it and sense memory have not distinct formal objects.

22 There is no evidence for essential superiority and much evidence for only accidental or individual variation within the powers or abilities of members of the human species. Excellent health is an organic condition just as sickness is; genius is intelligence; the most spectacular muscular virtuosity is still a matter of nerves and muscles. The basic nature and abilities, even if undeveloped, are the same in human beings.

Exercise 13, pages 70-71
Knowledge

1 Number 321	7 Number 327	14 Number 323
2 Number 320	8 Number 303	15 Number 326
3 Number 318	9 Number 304	16 Number 324
4 Number 305	10 Number 313	17 Number 319
5 Number 325	11 Number 310	18 Number 302
6 Numbers 302, 311, 325 (form)	12 Numbers 307-09	
	13 Number 314	

Exercise 14, pages 77-78
Material causality

In all problems in this exercise the mode of being of the recipient potency or the material cause in the broad sense of that cause shows that it has a real influence on the being of the result. It directly affects the form but indirectly affects the agent since the form produced by the agent is modified by the recipient potency. The recipient restricts, modifies, limits, individualizes, multiplies, helps, or handicaps the form.

1 As the axiom and correlative axioms on act and potency show, limitation and multiplication and specification of the act to determined limits depend on the potency.

2 We see the same kind of form, as of an elm, develop into very different elm trees, more and less perfect or deformed, healthy and unhealthy, and so on. The material component has much to do with these differences.

3 The material component of living plants depends much on soil. Good seed needs good ground. The Parable of the Sower has made this illustration of potency and its correlative in the receptivity of human minds and wills a classic instance of the principle.

4-5, 9, 11-12, 16

All forms of learning, of evaluation, of clearness of understanding depend to a great extent on the condition of the learner's faculties, habits, and past experience. Some learn quickly and others slowly in the same class and with seemingly the same external aids. Some have a wealth of background with which to coordinate and appraise new items of knowledge. Some are victims of their own prejudices, or of their voluntary unwillingness to see facts touching themselves in their objective light. Hence, Aristotle objects to young men as students of ethics because they lack sufficient experience of human life and because they are too moved by emotion to see ethical values truly. The sensory origin of our knowledge marks the analogical and often pictorial nature of our religious ideas.

6-7, 14

Not even the best doctor can cure every patient. The body is sometimes beyond the most intelligent diagnosis and most painstaking care. In mental disturbances the will of the patient seems incapable of cooperating, and so the attention and other dispositions of the patient are unfavorable to successful treatment. Problem 14 refers to the individual variations of health and illness. As Aristotle noted, the physician does not cure fevers but this and that man with a fever. Different patients with the same illness may need various differences in treatment.

8, 10

Consider the differences in the hardness of different woods, their coloring, their susceptibility to polish. Consider what effects can and cannot be achieved in marbles when compared with paints, and so on.

13 They vitally resist it and are not interested in evil.

15 Matter-form: as act to intention, or as experience to deliberate response. *confer* 233

17 Because the human soul itself is spiritual and so can be intrinsically modified only by something like its own nature, and not by something material of an essentially lower nature.

18 In the order of finite being or finite existence, the essence is as matter, the act of existing is as form. "Existence is the act of all acts" (St. Thomas).

Exercise 15, *pages* 83-85
Principles on stewardship

1 E

2 E balances H. Illicit if a substitute is possible or there is greater danger to father than to child.

3 B, F. It may succeed in a new trial.

4 C

5 E, if success is likely. Some authorities, however, would forbid this and answer H, J, K.

6 K, probably. The other fighter does not seem to be justified in risking injury in the ring.

7 G, K
8 G, H
9 C
10 B, F
11 J
12 B (probably proportionate temporary harm)
13 G (probably), H, and especially L
14 B
15 H (probably)
16 A, B, F
17 G, J, I (in intention), K, L
18 J (unless he is the victim of injustice)
19 A (functional mutilation), B
20 I, K
21 H, J, K
22 E
23 I
24 D
25 G, H, K

Exercise 17, pages 99-100
On rights

1 X	6 C	11 C	16 C	21 X	26 X
2 C	7 X	12 X	17 C	22 C	27 X
3 X	8 C	13 C	18 X	23 X	28 C
4 C	9 C	14 X	19 C	24 C	29 C
5 X	10 X	15 C	20 X	25 C	30 X

Exercise 18, pages 109-11
Truth in argument

1 Rule B in 534
2 "Too much" may mean an exaggerated conclusion and therefore, false. By Rules B and E, the proof itself then fails to prove. "Too much" may mean a somewhat irrelevant conclusion; and then the consistency and validity of the argument must be suspected.
3 Yes. For a true conclusion may accidentally come from false or irrelevant premises.
4 The conclusion may be certain for reasons other than those stated in the given premises.
5 Rule D.
6 This statement is correct. See also answer to 7.

7 What is proved is demonstrated as true and certain. What is disproved is refuted as false. What is unproved has not sufficient evidence for either its truth or falsity. Proof depends on evidence; so does disproof depend on the evidence presented in the reasoning. See Rule c2. Truth and falsity depend on conformity to reality itself, not necessarily on the evidence presented or omitted in the particular argument. *confer* 320 and 530

8 The statement is correct. What is said of truth and error is applicable to certainty and probability according to the arguments presented or other arguments not presented. *confer* 297

9 This may be so, especially as critics may judge the worth of the conclusion only on the merits of the arguments given for it by a writer. *confer* Rule c3

10 No. See Rule D, "not vice versa." The conclusion is merely unproved by the particular set of premises advanced.

11 Rule E, "not vice versa."

12 Rule F

13 Rule E, "not vice versa."

14 Rule B. We could, however, tell if all but one premise were evidently true. Or we can proceed by elimination of the true premise or premises.

15 All are legitimate. Methods D or E in combination with H is the strongest attack from the point of view of truth. The first technique to be adopted seems to depend on circumstances of the audience, clearer or briefer method, desired psychological or logical effectiveness, prevention of action on the opponent's conclusion, and so on. It is not the best rule to start always by attacking the conclusion, though this must be the aim in all refutation.

16 This is the technique in Problem 15E.

17 Disagreement is supposedly rational, and therefore it implies agreement on some premises from which men can reason to an agreed true conclusion. Hence, it is humane as well as logically skillful to save whatever one can of the opponent's premises or meanings in his premises.

18 There is this difference that fruits depend on the tree as a cause; but a true conclusion is not caused by false premises, but is a chance event from the arrangement of the premises rather than from their truth.

19 This is like the technique in Problem 15G. What is proposed as good should be good in all respects. Or again, since the true and the good are ultimately identical, what is opposed to the good is also opposed to genuine truth.

20 True. See also 532. Rule c in 534 does not say that only one false conclusion may follow, especially as there may be a variety of premises. A

classic instance is provided by the Christological heresies. For example, Nestorius reasoned:

> There are as many persons as there are natures. *False*
> But there are two natures in Christ. *True*
> Therefore, there are two persons in Christ. *False*

And Eutyches twenty years later argued:

> There are as many persons as there are natures. *False*
> But there is only one person in Christ. *True*
> Therefore, there is only one nature in Christ. *False*

21 No. See c1-3. Scholastics accept the conclusion on quite different arguments and do not think that truths should be supported by bad, inadequate reasons.

22 (1) Ends do not justify means. *confer* 237 (2) Ends give their goodness to otherwise indifferent means. (3) Effectiveness of means is relative to ends; but bad means do not accomplish moral good. (4) From the logical point of view, means must not be regarded as consequences flowing logically from ends. Hence, the technique of 15G may not be adopted in arguing from justice of ends to the unrelated question of the justice of the means.

23 The enthymeme has a hidden major premise: "All right causes always win." Hence, it also refers to future victories of such causes. If the premise is granted, the statement in the problem could follow. But the premise is challengeable and maybe the rightness of "our" cause is challengeable. Thus a conclusion referring to the future can be met usually only by challenging the premises or the intrinsic possibility of the conclusion.

24 This refutation of idealism and relativism is the technique in Problem 15G. Like all negative proofs, however, it may not give much light.

25 Rule c2.

26 A The technique in 15G. B The techniques in 15B and c. c The technique in 15D. The last is the best and the most direct refutation.

27 Yes. Rule c1.

28 Yes. Guilt is a fact. See Rules c3 and e, "not vice versa." The reasoning of the detectives may also be wrong, particularly as involving incomplete disjunctions about the parties responsible for the clues.

29 Rules e and b.

30 This is a variation of Problems 19 and 18. Also notice that techniques are judged by results, not by theoretical considerations. The same techniques may be used by persons with widely differing theories of human nature, of human disease, of human desires, and so on.

Will and human acts

1 Number 554, corollary	11 Numbers 241-46
2 Number 568	12 Number 561
3 Number 552	13 Number 557
4 Number 554	14 Number 557
5 Number 555	15 Number 561
6 Number 558	16 Number 551
7 Number 229	17 Number 556
8 Number 247	18 Numbers 241-42
9 Number 558	19 Number 568
10 Number 566	20 Number 563

Exercise 20, *pages* 117-18
Use of principles in natural theology

1 A contingency, universal consent, conscience; and any proof in as far as it involves the insufficiency of an infinite series of like causes
  B order of causes; contingency
  C motion
  D order; finality; happiness
  E grades of being
2 Number 84, criteria C-D, F, and in a sense H. See example worked in Exercise 5 on identifying real distinctions.
3 Number 14; Thomistic theses 3-4
4 The following apply with due analogy for God's way of knowing and for identity of being, intellect, act of intellect, and will in God: 302, 304-05, 308, 311-13, 318-19, 324-25. The following do not apply: 303, 306-07, 309-10, 314-17, 320-23, 326-30.
5 Number 350. As a perfectly intelligent cause, He creates according to His ideas and with perfect wisdom and complete knowledge.
6 Number 566. God needs no good other than His own infinite goodness. He has power to do anything. He knows all possible things before He chooses to make any of them. He knows that He needs none of them. The primary object of His love is His own goodness, not finite goods imitating Him.
7 A Number 37, analogy of being. God's essence is His existence, is infinite, pure actuality, and so on. In no other being is there such identity of essence with existence, nor pure and infinite actuality of existence and all perfections.
  B Analogy of cause and effect: 113, 104F. God causes the being, not merely the form nor the changes; He causes all things; He causes without help of any material cause.

c Analogy of infinite and finite: 162, 400, 409, 38.

8 Numbers 27, 29

9 A to test whether the event is a miraculous exception
  B the need of a cause higher than a natural one
  c the historical fact of the occurrence of the unusual event
  D (1) a higher than natural good is accomplished by the miracle; (2) the exceptional occurrence is passing; natural laws continue to operate

10 priorities of nature and of excellence

11 only as real principle and never as matter or form; but as efficient cause, end, and exemplar of being, natures, operations, truth, goodness, grace, life, law, and especially of persons

12 Number 95. God as subsistent being, as being in the most proper and unrestricted sense, gives being; He alone gives being; He gives it to all things. His power or causality is identified with His being. He makes all like Himself in being; no other cause produces being.

13 Origin of our knowledge of God dependent on sense and analogies with sense; approach to knowledge of God is through effects imperfectly like Him or in the lower grade of analogous perfections; God is not the connatural object of our intellects; no finite species can represent the infinite, but we need a species to know.

14 love, 326

Exercise 21, *pages* 124-25
Suggestions for study of the Thomistic theses

2 A metaphysics: 1-9
  B philosophy of nature: 8-14
  c philosophy of man: 13-21
  D epistemology: 18-20
  E natural theology: 3-4, 22-24

3 The general order moves from metaphysics through other branches as indicated in answer 2. The position moves from general discussions of potency and act and their composition to the types of beings, uncreated and created being; in created being, from angels to natural bodies to living bodies to man; in man, from nature to soul to powers of intellect and of will, to use of intellect in the knowledge of God, to God's existence, then His essence, then His prerogative as Creator and universal cooperating cause.

4 A no potency in God; hence, no limitation, composition, multiplicity in the divine order of being
  B potency in all creatures; hence, limitation, a twofold composition at least, and multiplicity

c angels: composition of existence with essence, of substance with accidents

D See 8-9, 13-14.

E See 5, 8.

F See 17.

G See 11.

H See 13-14.

5 See 2-3, 22-24.

6 two kinds of analogy mentioned in 4

7 Check key words in *Index to Principles*.

8 A Numbers 2, 16, 23   D Numbers 12, 14, 18

   B Numbers 2-4, 24   E Numbers 13-16

   C Numbers 7-8   F Numbers 19-20

9 A immediately evident: 1; 2, first sentence.

   B dependent in whole or in part on previous theses in the list

     3 dependent on 2   13 partly dependent on 8

     4 dependent on 2-3   14 partly dependent on 13

     5 dependent on 3   19 partly dependent on 18

     7 dependent on 3 and 5   20 partly dependent on 11 and 19

     8 partly dependent on 2   23 dependent on 2-3

     11 dependent on 2   24 partly dependent on 2-4, 23

   C need independent proof in whole or in part: 6, 8, 10, 12-22, 24

10 A signs of real distinction: opposite properties, causality, separability, adequate distinction of concepts

   B freedom from potencies and various limitations; different mode of causality

11 Aristotelian evidences in 1-2, 8-10, 13-14, 17-19, 21 in part, 22 in the first proof

12 See Supplement IV.

13 existence of the human soul, its status as form, its immortality and spirituality; freedom of will; existence of angels; demonstrability of God's existence from creatures; God creates and concurs

14 some notable omissions: all doctrines of ethics and political philosophy; much of the doctrine on final causes; theory of demonstration; sensory appetites and internal senses; love; providence; specification by formal objects; habits; truth and error and other epistemological questions; nature of the judgment; miracles; and so on

15 safeguards against:

   A pantheism, especially 3-4, 24

   B agnosticism, especially 18-20, 22

   C materialism, especially 7, 15, 17-18, 22

   D human dualism, especially 9, 16

Index to principles